Good News for
All People

Good News for All People

P. G. Mathew

GRACE & GLORY
MINISTRIES

GRACE & GLORY MINISTRIES
Davis, California

© 2012 by P. G. Mathew. Published by Grace and Glory Ministries, Davis, California. Printed in the United States of America. All rights reserved. No part of this book may be reproduced or transmitted in any form or by any means, electronic or mechanical, including photocopying, recording, or by an information storage and retrieval system—except by a reviewer who may quote brief passages in a review to be printed in a magazine, newspaper, or on the Web—without permission in writing from the publisher. For information, please contact Grace and Glory Ministries, gvcc@gracevalley.org.

ISBN: 978-0-9771149-6-2

Library of Congress Control Number: 2012944630

Contents

About the Author

The Reverend P. G. Mathew, who holds three graduate degrees in theology from Central and Westminster theological seminaries (USA), is the founder and senior minister of Grace Valley Christian Center in California. Originally a scientist from India, he is also a former professor of Greek and systematic theology and has traveled widely for Christian mission interests. He is the author of *The Normal Church Life* (1 John), *Victory in Jesus* (Joshua), *The Wisdom of Jesus* (The Sermon on the Mount), *Muscular Christianity* (Hebrews), *Romans 1–8: The Gospel Freedom*, and several other books. He is also the founder and president of Grace Valley Christian Academy. For more information, visit *www.gracevalley.org*.

Introduction

"The gospel is the power of God unto salvation for everyone who believes" (Rom. 1:16). The word *gospel* means "good news." This good news is embodied in Jesus Christ, the eternal Son of God. He is the one sent by God the Father as Savior.

For whom is this good news? It is for all people. Before he ascended, the risen Lord Jesus commissioned his disciples: "But you will receive power when the Holy Spirit comes on you; and you will be my witnesses in Jerusalem, and in all Judea and Samaria, and to the ends of the earth" (Acts 1:8). This offer of salvation is for everyone.

There is also a sense in which this good news is only for one kind of people—bad people. Those who see themselves as good and righteous will never see their need for Christ. Only lost sinners see their need for a Savior. This good news, then, is for everyone, because "all have sinned and fall short of the glory of God" (Rom. 3:23). Christ declared that he came not to save the righteous but sinners (Matt. 9:12–13). Christ has come to save his people from their sins.

But if you think you are a good person, then this good news is not for you. For those who are good in their own eyes (i.e., self-righteous), God has only bad news. The bad news is that you are not as good as you think you are. The path of the self-righteous leads only to destruction (Prov. 14:12).

There is hope only for those who see themselves as sinners. As Jonathan Edwards preached, we are all "sinners in the hands of an angry God." God is holy and just, so he necessarily hates and judges all wickedness, rebellion, and sin. And the punishment our sin deserves is eternal death. "The wages of sin is death. . ." (Rom. 6:23a).

God has good news of great joy for all sinners! And since no one is righteous, not even one (Rom. 3:10), this means that God indeed has good news for all people! Not only is it true that the wages of sin is death, but Paul also goes on to say that "the gift of God is eternal life in Christ Jesus our Lord" (Rom. 6:23b). God gave his only begotten Son to save sinners out of a world that already stood condemned.

Nowhere in the Bible is the gospel of God more thoroughly and clearly expressed than in Paul's letter to the Romans. And nowhere in the book of Romans does Paul proclaim the good news as lucidly as he does in Romans 3:21–26. Here is the very heart of the gospel.

My prayer is that God would open your heart to receive his message of salvation, which this book articulates. I pray that the Holy Spirit would first convict you of your sin and lead you to cry out, "What must I do to be saved?" Then by faith you can receive God's good news for all people, as declared by Paul in Acts 16:31, "Believe in the Lord Jesus, and you will be saved."

1

Divine Diagnosis
of Man's Heart

⁹What shall we conclude then? Are we any better? Not at all! We have already made the charge that Jews and Gentiles alike are all under sin. ¹⁰As it is written:

"There is no one righteous, not even one; ¹¹there is no one who understands, no one who seeks God. ¹²All have turned away, they have together become worthless; there is no one who does good, not even one."

¹³"Their throats are open graves; their tongues practice deceit." "The poison of vipers is on their lips."

¹⁴"Their mouths are full of cursing and bitterness."

¹⁵"Their feet are swift to shed blood; ¹⁶ruin and misery mark their ways, ¹⁷and the way of peace they do not know."

¹⁸"There is no fear of God before their eyes."

¹⁹Now we know that whatever the law says, it says to those who are under the law, so that every mouth may be silenced and the whole world held accountable to God. ²⁰Therefore no one will be declared righteous in his sight by observing the law; rather, through the law we become conscious of sin.

Romans 3:9–20

1

We cannot understand reality—why we need salvation and why Jesus Christ came to accomplish our salvation—unless we first understand and believe the Genesis account of man's creation, fall, and redemption. The first three chapters of the Bible teach us that Adam, the head of the entire human family, sinned against his Creator. This act of rebellion and its subsequent effect on the human race is known as the Fall. As a consequence, all men now have by nature a depraved mind. The apostle Paul emphasizes the very same truth when he writes: *"Jews and Gentiles alike are all under sin"* (v. 9). He is speaking of the universality of sin. He has proven that Gentiles are sinners (Rom 1:18–32). And he has proven that Jews are also sinners (Rom 2:1–3:8). There is no difference. Every man is under sin, meaning "under the power of sin." Sin is personified as the master, and man is enslaved to sin. We cannot get out from under the dominion of sin on our own.

In Genesis we read, "The LORD saw how great man's wickedness on earth had become, and that every inclination of the thoughts of his heart was only evil all the time" (Gen. 6:5). This speaks about three aspects of sin: it is internal, pervasive, and continuous. This describes the total depravity of man. Jeremiah declares, "The heart is deceitful above all things and beyond cure. Who can understand it?" (Jer. 17:9). The answer is that only God can.

This is God's diagnosis of the human heart. Jesus says sin and uncleanness are not external, but internal; they are problems of our hearts: "For from within, out of men's hearts, come evil thoughts, sexual immorality, theft, murder, adultery, greed, malice, deceit, lewdness, envy, slander, arrogance and folly. All these evils come from inside and make a man 'unclean'" (Mark 7:21–23). Paul also tells us that we are by nature dead in trespasses and sins, and under the rule of Satan (Eph. 2:1–3).

All people are sinners; there is no exception. That is why the Bible is relevant to everyone. In seminary I was told that when I preach the gospel, all manner of people will be listening to me—educated or uneducated, rich or poor—but I must not worry. They all are sinners who must hear the gospel so that they may be saved. God's word does not show favoritism. It levels everyone.

Paul gives ample proof from the Bible to prove the truth of our depravity, citing multiple verses from the Old Testament. He only needs to cite the scriptures, for the Jews understood that the Scriptures are the final authority.

1. "There is no one righteous, not even one" (v. 10; Eccl. 7:20). God demands perfect conformity to his law. But since the Fall, all have become twisted in their minds; there is no one who is upright in thought and life. J. B. Phillips says, "No man can justify himself before God by a perfect performance of the Law's demands—indeed, the Law is the straight-edge that shows us how crooked we are" (Rom. 3:20, Phillips translation).[1]

This is the reason many people do not want to read the Bible. Every theologian and higher critic who criticizes the Bible is revealing what the Bible affirms, that we are sinners who cannot tolerate what the Bible has to say about us. And if we ourselves are not reading the Bible, it is for the same reason: we do not want to be confronted with our sin. Either this Book will keep us from sin, or sin will keep us from this Book. Because we are sinners, we tend to hate the Bible because it exposes our wickedness. Yet that is the very reason we should read it! It is like going to a doctor to have our problem diagnosed so that we can be healed. In the same way, we must read the Bible to know exactly what our problem is. And not only does the Bible tell us our problem, but it also tells how we can be saved.

So Paul says no man is righteous. Martyn Lloyd-Jones says, "The best man, the noblest, the most learned, the most philanthropic, the greatest idealist, the greatest

---

1   http://www.ccel.org/bible/phillips/CP06Romans.htm

thinker, say what you like about him—there has never been a man who can stand up to the test of the law. Drop your plumb-line, and he is not true to it."[2] This is why we should read the Bible from beginning to end.

2. *"There is no one who understands"* (v. 11; Ps. 14:2). How often do we tell others how much we understand! Only God knows all things, and he has here revealed his truth about man's condition: "No one understands." This is a universal condition; there is no exception. Because even our minds were corrupted by the Fall (the noetic effect of sin), no one understands God, man, or creation. Without knowing God first, we cannot understand even the simplest thing. In fact, most people see truth as lie and lie as truth, and deny the infinite, personal God. They do so because they lack spiritual understanding. They believe in a closed system where God is not permitted. They are like the Sadducees, who denied the resurrection, angels, evil spirits, heaven, hell, and eternal judgment. Irrational materialists believe in evolution but not creation. Paul says that the natural man does not understand things that are spiritual; they are foolishness to him (1 Cor. 2:14). Spiritual things make him fume and fight.

Natural man is not wise, because he does not fear God. The fear of God is the beginning of wisdom. Paul says about the unbeliever's mind: "You must no longer live as the Gentiles do, in the futility of their thinking. They are darkened in their understanding and separated from the life of God because of the ignorance that is in them due to the hardening of their hearts. Having lost all sensitivity, they have given themselves over to sensuality so as to indulge in every kind of impurity, with a continual lust for more" (Eph. 4:17–19). Elsewhere Paul says, "The god of this age has blinded the minds of unbelievers, so that they cannot

---

2   D. Martyn Lloyd-Jones, *Romans*, vol. 2, *An Exposition of Romans 2:1–3:20: The Righteous Judgment of God* (Grand Rapids: Zondervan, 1989), 198.

see the light of the gospel of the glory of Christ, who is the image of God" (2 Cor. 4:4). People hate the Bible and Jesus Christ because they are darkened in their understanding.

3. *"No one who seeks God"* (v. 11; Ps. 14:2). Not only is man's mind twisted, but his will is also twisted. He will not seek the true God—the Father, Son, and Holy Spirit—the God of the Scriptures. That does not mean he is not religious. In fact, he is a connoisseur of the false religions of idolatry, the demon-inspired religions that God abhors. He will worship creation, demons, trees, snakes, bulls, birds, and man. But he will not worship the true and living God. Natural man is an enemy of God (Rom. 5:10; 8:7).

4. *"All have turned away"* (v. 12; Ps. 14:3). Again, notice, there is no exception. All have turned away from God's path, the way of truth, to the broad way of the lie. Every man is on the way to hell: "The way of the wicked will perish" (Ps. 1:6). The Greek text says all have turned away deliberately. In our depravity we say, "I do not want truth or light. I do not want to know what my problems are. I hate God's way!" Isaiah says, "We all, like sheep, have gone astray, each of us has turned to his own way" (Isa. 53:6).

5. *"They have together become worthless"* (v. 12; Ps. 14:3). This, again, is universal. Every person has become worthless and useless to God. They have become like milk that has gone sour, or like meat that has become rotten. Such people are useless to God and everyone else. Through God's common grace, man can still do civic good, like discovering new medicines, but he is worthless in things that matter ultimately.

The Conduct of Sinful Man

Having described the condition of man, Paul continues his scriptural proofs as he examines the conduct of sinful man.

6. *"There is no one who does good, not even one"* (v. 12; Ps. 14:3). People like to parade their self-righteousness,

5

but Isaiah said all human righteousness is like filthy rags (Isa. 64:6). Paul likened it to dung (Phil. 3:8). All works done by a sinner before he trusts in God are dead works, done for man's own glory, not for the glory of God. A good work is done by a believer for God's glory.

First Samuel 15 describes how Saul fought the Amalekites. When he returned from the battle, he got up early and went to build a monument. This monument, however, was not to the Lord but to Saul himself. Unbelievers perform works for their own glory, not God's. But Jesus says, "What is highly valued among men is detestable in God's sight" (Luke 16:15).

7. "Their throats are open graves" (v. 13; Ps. 5:9). The throat of a sinner is like a grave that is opened up: a stench comes out of it. This expression can also mean they will eat or bury people. Jesus declares, "Out of the overflow of the heart the mouth speaks" (Matt. 12:34). Such people emit a stench from within them that destroys people.

8. "Their tongues practice deceit" (v. 13; Ps. 5:9). This simply means sinners lie continuously and use flattery to get their way. We have heard parents, philosophers, politicians, professors, pastors, advertisers, and many others lie. We have heard the lies of evolution, the innate goodness of man, and the equality of all religions. Sinners are not only deceived but they also deceive others, especially through words. Think of preachers who preach salvation without repentance. They will say, "Our God is nice. I know you do not like repentance, so I will just preach salvation without repentance, justification without sanctification, faith without faithfulness, a God who is love but not holy, and a Jesus who is Savior but not Lord." Such lying preachers are even more dangerous than lying professors or philosophers.

9. "The poison of vipers is on their lips" (v. 13; Ps. 140:3). Think of the counsel Job's wife gave her husband: "Curse God and die!" (Job 2:9). That is real poison, aimed to kill

a person. How many people use their tongues to deceive others! They may use flattery and speak many nice words, but their intent is to destroy. Lloyd-Jones writes about this analogy:

> This is a very fine description in a zoological sense. The adder, or viper, which is so harmful and so poisonous, has the poison concealed in a little bag at the root of the lips. This little bag is under the upper jaw of the adder close to some fangs which lie in a horizontal position. When the adder is about to pounce upon a victim he puts back his head and as he does so, these teeth or fangs drop down and he bites the victim. As he is biting with the fangs one of them presses the bag that is full of poison and into the wound is injected this venom, this poison that is going to kill the victim! So the Bible gives an exact scientific description of how the adder kills by means of his poison.[3]

10. *"Their mouths are full of cursing and bitterness"* (v. 14; Ps. 10:7). The cursing and bitterness overflow from their cursed and bitter hearts.

11. *"Their feet are swift to shed blood"* (v. 15; Isa. 59:7). The history of the world is a history of killing and murder. The devil is behind all murder. Jesus said, "You belong to your father, the devil, and you want to carry out your father's desire. He was a murderer from the beginning, not holding to the truth, for there is no truth in him. When he lies, he speaks his native language, for he is a liar and the father of lies" (John 8:44). Elsewhere he explained, "The thief comes only to steal and kill and destroy; I have come that they may have life, and have it to the full" (John 10:10).

12. *"Ruin and misery mark their ways"* (v. 16; Isa. 59:7). The wicked are like tsunamis, hurricanes, cyclones, and earthquakes. We see them coming and going, leaving

---

3   Lloyd-Jones, *Romans*, vol. 2, *Righteous Judgment of God*, 211.

destruction and misery behind. The history of kingdoms and civilizations is a history of ruin and misery.

13. *"The way of peace they do not know"* (v. 17; Isa. 59:8). "'There is no peace,' says my God, 'for the wicked'" (Isa. 57:21). Jesus Christ is the Prince of peace. A man outside of Jesus is a man without peace. He is restless like the waves of the sea.

The Cause of Man's Miserable Condition

What is the cause of all this misery, sin, and wickedness? Again, Paul quotes from the Scriptures: *"There is no fear of God before their eyes"* (v. 18; Ps. 36:1).[4]

As David declares, "The fool says in his heart, 'There is no God'" (Ps. 14:1). All the deeds of wicked men are done without any God-consciousness. It is fear of God that keeps us from sinning (Exod. 20:20). He who fears God shuns evil, as Joseph did, saying, "How then could I do such a wicked thing and sin against God?" (Gen. 39:9). The fear of God kept him from sinning. Daniel also refused to sin out of fear of God, as did his three friends, who would not worship the golden image.

Above all, Jesus Christ always feared God, even when tempted most severely. Isaiah said the Spirit of the fear of the Lord would be upon him (Isa. 11:2). The Holy Spirit also causes us to fear the Lord. David said, "I have set the LORD always before me. Because he is at my right hand, I will not be shaken" (Ps. 16:8). He is speaking about a God-conscious life, saying, "I have deliberately set the Lord before me so that he governs my thoughts, words, and deeds."

When Paul says there is no fear of God before their eyes, this does not mean every sinner is as bad as he could possibly be. Rather, it means that no action of a sinner can ever receive divine approbation. Even the best actions

---

4   Ironically, when we do not fear God, we fear everything.

of a sinner are done for his own glory most of all. Can we ever come to God and say, "I did this or that; therefore, you should justify me"? Absolutely not! Jesus understood this and called such people "a wicked and adulterous generation" (Matt. 12:39; 16:4).

The Conclusion

Paul concludes this section, *"Now we know that whatever the law says, it says to those who are under the law,"* that is, *"in the sphere of the law"* (v. 19). If you have a Bible, it is speaking to you. The Jews were given the Old Testament, so they were in the sphere of the law. The Gentiles were as well, for they were given the revelation of God through creation, and the works of the law were written in their hearts. Every man, therefore, is under God's law and knows God; yet he refuses to glorify God and give thanks to him. Instead, he exchanges truth for a lie and worships creation. But the word of God is living. God is speaking to us; are we listening?

What is the purpose of the law? Paul continues, *"so that every mouth may be silenced"* (v. 19). The picture is that of being in the courtroom of God. God is the judge and we are the defendants. We are given time to speak but we cannot: our mouths are shut. We know we are guilty as charged; therefore, we cannot speak, because we have no defense. That is what will happen when we face God.

The second reason Paul gives is *"so that . . . the whole world [may be] held accountable to God"* (v. 19). Every man is under divine judgment and is without excuse. Elsewhere Paul writes especially about the Gentiles, "For since the creation of the world God's invisible qualities— his eternal power and divine nature—have been clearly seen, being understood from what has been made, so that men are without excuse" (Rom. 1:20). He said to the Jews, "You, therefore, have no excuse" (Rom. 2:1). Every mouth, therefore, is stopped and the whole world is under divine judgment. We all stand guilty before God.

This is the divine diagnosis. No one can be declared righteous in God's sight by observing the law. The reason is that no man can observe the law as God demands because every man is a sinner. Jesus spoke of a Pharisee who prayed to himself, parading his self-righteousness. He was saying, "I have no use for Jesus Christ or the cross. I can save myself." But he went home condemned (Luke 18:9–14). Paul also once paraded his righteousness, saying, "As for legalistic righteousness, [I was] faultless" (Phil. 3:6). But when God apprehended him, Paul found out his righteousness was dung.

The law condemns us. Jesus said to those who were relying on their own works, "Away from me, you evildoers!" (Matt. 7:23). The psalmist says, "No one living is righteous before you" (Ps. 143:2). It is impossible to save ourselves.

What, then, is the purpose of the law? It is through the law that we receive knowledge of sin. God's law is the mirror for our lives. That is why we must read it all the time. It shows our sins. The law does not forgive our sins or justify us. In fact, the law makes sin worse by revealing, condemning, and aggravating our sin. A mirror shows dirt on our faces, but it cannot wash our faces clean. We need Christ to make us clean, and the law points to Christ, the Savior of the world. In other words, the law is the straight-edge that shows how crooked we are. Jesus alone can make us straight.

This, then, is the divine diagnosis of our heart: its condition, its conduct, its cause, and the conclusion. Knowing no one can save himself, is there any hope for a sinful man? Is there any effective medicine for a sinner? Can I obtain a new heart?

The answer is yes. Not only does the Bible reveal our problem, but it also gives us the remedy. In the next passage, Romans 3:21–26, Paul gives us the prescription that will heal us. As Paul declares, "I am not ashamed of the gospel, because it is the power of God for the salvation of everyone who believes: first for the Jew, then for the Gentile. For in the gospel a righteousness from God is revealed, a righteousness that is by faith from first to last, just as it is written: 'The righteous will live by faith'" (Rom. 1:16–17).

The publican simply said, "God, have mercy on me, a sinner," and he went home justified (Luke 18:13–14). The thief from the cross said, "Jesus, remember me when you come into your kingdom," and Jesus responded, "Today you will be with me in paradise" (Luke 23:42–43). Jesus came to seek and save lost sinners like us.

> Amazing grace, how sweet the sound
> that saved a wretch like me!

If Jesus Christ has taken us out of the dominion, power, and mastery of sin and placed us under the power of grace and the lordship of Christ, we can all go out justified, walking and leaping and praising God.

Application Questions

1) What does the historical Fall of Adam and Eve (Genesis 1–3) teach us about ourselves?

2) According to Romans 3:9–20, is there anyone who can say, "I deserve to go to heaven"?

3) If you were to die tonight and come before God, and he were to ask you, "Why should I let you into my heaven?" what would be your answer?

2

Justification by Grace

²¹But now a righteousness from God, apart from law, has been made known, to which the Law and the Prophets testify. ²²This righteousness from God comes through faith in Jesus Christ to all who believe. There is no difference, ²³for all have sinned and fall short of the glory of God, ²⁴and are justified freely by his grace through the redemption that came by Christ Jesus. ²⁵God presented him as a sacrifice of atonement, through faith in his blood. He did this to demonstrate his justice, because in his forbearance he had left the sins committed beforehand unpunished— ²⁶he did it to demonstrate his justice at the present time, so as to be just and the one who justifies those who have faith in Jesus.

Romans 3:21–26

Leon Morris regards Romans 3:21–26 as possibly the most important single paragraph ever written.[1] Luther calls it the chief point of the whole Bible. This passage speaks about three aspects of salvation: justification, redemption, and propitiation. This chapter will focus on justification by grace.

Increasingly, self-identified "Bible-believing" people report that they believe that there are many ways to eternal life. This directly contradicts the biblical view

---

1   Leon Morris, *The Epistle to the Romans* (Grand Rapids: Eerdmans, reprinted 1992), 173.

that salvation is found in Jesus Christ alone. Jesus himself proclaims, "I am the way and the truth and the life. No one comes to the Father except through me" (John 14:6). Peter also declares, "Salvation is found in no one else, for there is no other name under heaven given to men by which we must be saved" (Acts 4:12).

Dr. John Stott says, "No other system, ideology or religion proclaims a free forgiveness and a new life to those who have done nothing to deserve it but a lot to deserve judgment instead."[2] Let us examine this great passage that opens for us knowledge of the way of eternal salvation.

A New Era

Paul begins, "But now . . ." (v. 21). This "now" is contrasted with the former times of divine salvation. Earlier Paul spoke of the wrath of God being revealed against all godlessness and wickedness of men who suppress the truth in wicked deeds. He proved that all have sinned and are under God's wrath, that there is none righteous, none who seek God or do good, and that there is no fear of God before the eyes of man (Rom. 1:18–3:20).

Later in this epistle he explains that man is a powerless, ungodly sinner. Man is an enemy of God, for the very heart of sin is enmity toward God. His mind is hostile to God, and he cannot please God. Guilty and hell-bound, man cannot save himself by his own good works.

So Paul writes, "Therefore, no one will be declared righteous in his sight by observing the law" (v. 20). We must be saved by another. The mighty God, against whom all men have sinned, must save us because there is no other savior. But, thank God, a new era has begun. In the fullness of time, the era of grace and divine

---

2   John R. W. Stott, *Romans: God's Good News for the World* (Downers Grove, IL: InterVarsity, 1994), 118.

salvation came in Jesus Christ. Paul declares, "But when the time had fully come, God sent his Son, born of a woman, born under law, to redeem those under law, that we might receive the full rights of sons" (Gal. 4:4–5). He also proclaimed to the Athenians, "In the past God overlooked such ignorance, but now he commands all people everywhere to repent" (Acts 17:30).

A new era of grace has come—the era of the Messiah. The Hebrews writer says, "Now [Christ] has appeared once for all at the end of the ages to do away with sin by the sacrifice of himself" (Heb. 9:26). We are living in this "now," when we sinners can call upon the name of Jesus and be set free from slavery to sin, guilt, condemnation, Satan, death, and hell. Paul writes, "Now is the time of God's favor, now is the day of salvation" (2 Cor. 6:2). Today is the day of fulfillment of God's promise of a Savior—a promise first made in Genesis 3:15 and now fulfilled in Jesus Christ.

A Righteousness from God

Paul then explains what is happening in this new era: *"But now a righteousness from God, apart from law, has been made known"* (v. 21). This righteousness was revealed once for all in the life, death, and resurrection of Christ. Jesus died for our sins and was raised for our justification (Rom. 4:25). As Moses lifted up the brazen serpent in the wilderness for the healing of all who had been bitten by poisonous serpents, so Christ was lifted up on the cross to manifest a righteousness from God that alone can meet our need. The gospel reveals this righteousness from God.

This righteousness of God is apart from the law-works of man. The Jews of Jesus' day misunderstood the way of salvation. They taught that people could earn salvation by meritorious good works done in obedience to the Mosaic law. Jesus gave an example of such thinking: "To some who were confident of their own righteousness and looked down on everybody else, Jesus told this parable: 'Two men went up to the temple to pray, one a Pharisee and the other a tax collector. The Pharisee stood up and prayed about himself: "God, I thank you that I am not like other men—robbers, evildoers, adulterers—or even like this tax collector. I fast twice a week and give a tenth of all I get"'" (Luke 18:9–12).

Judaism taught salvation by self, not by the Messiah. The Messiah came to his own people but they rejected him, thinking they did not need a Savior. This is still true today. But the Mosaic law was never intended to save anyone. Paul writes, "Therefore no one will be declared righteous in his sight by observing the law; rather, through the law we become conscious of sin" (Rom. 3:20). To those who want to glory in their self-righteousness and human merit, he says, "Law brings wrath" (Rom. 4:15). In other words, the wrath of God shall be poured out on the one who depends on the law. The law aggravates and increases sin: "The law was added so that the trespass might increase" (Rom. 5:20).

Man, who is a slave of sin, cannot keep God's law perfectly. Paul writes in Romans 3:9 and 7:14 that we are "under sin," meaning we are so much under the control and power of sin that we cannot deliver ourselves from its grip. God himself had to deliver us through his Son.

The angel told Joseph, "You are to give him the name Jesus, because he will save his people from their sins" (Matt. 1:21). Jesus Christ saves us, not *in* our sins, but *from* our sins—from their power and dominion over us. "If the Son sets you free, you will be free indeed" (John 8:36). That is why we must come to Jesus without any claim of merit. Jesus saves only those who know they are sinners and cannot save themselves. Any merit-based plea will condemn us.

Paul describes God as one who justifies the ungodly (Rom. 4:5). Are you ungodly? Are you a sinner? Are you loaded down with guilt? Then come to Jesus. He will do what is humanly impossible and save you. With God all things are possible.

Not a New Salvation

Look again at verse 21: "*But now a righteousness from God, apart from law, has been made known, to which the Law and the Prophets testify.*" The entire Old Testament spoke about a salvation by grace through faith. Abraham, David, and all other Old Testament saints were justified by grace through faith, as Paul discusses in Romans 4 and as we read in the book of Hebrews. Habakkuk said the just shall live by faith (Hab. 2:4). Paul later quotes David, "Blessed are they whose transgressions are forgiven, whose sins are covered. Blessed is the man whose sin the Lord will never count against him" (Rom. 4:7–8; Ps. 32:1–2). The idea here is that our sin will be counted against another.

The Old Testament sacrificial system pointed to justification by grace through faith. Jesus himself spoke of this: "'Did not the Christ have to suffer these things and then enter his glory?' And beginning with Moses and all the Prophets, he explained to them what was said in all the Scriptures concerning himself. . . . He told them, 'This is what is written: The Christ will suffer and rise from the dead on the third day, and repentance and forgiveness of sins will be preached in his name to all nations'" (Luke 24:26–27, 46–47).

There is continuity in the way of salvation between the Old and the New Testament; the entire Old Testament speaks of this righteousness of God apart from the law. This way of justification is not a new idea; God saves sinners by grace through faith in all dispensations. The Bible never teaches a merit-based self-salvation. The Pharisee who prided in his works of the law went home condemned (Luke 18:14).

Justified Freely by His Grace

Sinners who believe in Christ *"are justified freely by his grace"* (v. 24). The words "righteousness," "justify," and "just" appear seven times in this passage. The righteousness of God is a justifying, divine, God-given righteousness that God demands of us. This objective righteousness of Christ meets our need. The Greek text says *"being* justified," meaning one sinner at a time is given the righteousness of God that we read about in verse 21. God gives us his righteousness, we receive it, and we are justified.

Question 70 of the Westminster Larger Catechism asks, "What is justification?" The answer: "Justification is an act of God's free grace unto sinners, in which he pardoneth all their sins, accepteth and accounteth their persons righteous in his sight; not for anything wrought in them, or done by them, but only for the perfect obedience and full satisfaction of Christ, by God imputed to them, and received by faith alone."

Imagine a condemned criminal waiting to be executed for his crime being told he is free to go home to his wife, children, and friends. He can do so because an innocent person who loved the criminal has agreed to be executed for his crime in his stead. This is justification. Barabbas went home, while Jesus was crucified.

Justification is the language of the heavenly courtroom. Deuteronomy 25:1 says, "When men have a dispute, they are to take it to court and the judges will decide the case, acquitting the innocent and condemning the guilty." Yet in Romans 4:5 Paul speaks of "God who justifies the wicked." This seems to be a contradiction, for how can God justify the wicked? A judge should declare the innocent as innocent and the guilty as guilty. His business is not to make people innocent or guilty. We are guilty, ungodly, wicked enemies of God, yet God pronounces us just.

First, we must realize that when God justifies us, he is *declaring* us to be righteous, not *making* us righteous within. Justification is not sanctification. Dr. Stott says, "[God] is pronouncing [sinners] legally righteous, free from any liability to the broken law, because he himself in his Son has borne the penalty for their law-breaking."[3]

Justification is God's legal declaration that our sins are forgiven and that God's righteousness is ours. God gives us a new legal standing. God's legal declaration is irrevocable and irreversible. Who can challenge what the Supreme Judge of the universe has pronounced?

The justified are not automatically changed within, but God, who declares us to be legally righteous forever, will also see to it that we are changed within. In fact, if we do not change, we are not justified. Dr. Boice says, "Actual [or experimental] righteousness does follow on justification—so closely that we are correct in saying that if it does not, the one involved is not justified."[4] In other words, if the justified person is not being sanctified, as evidenced in obedience and godliness, then he is not justified. Justification necessarily leads to sanctification; we are made righteous progressively within. Our good works prove our prior justification.

Roman Catholics confuse justification and sanctification, and imputed and imparted righteousness. They teach that justification makes us righteous within, but that righteousness is based partly on God's works and partly on ours. Such theology cannot give us assurance of salvation, because our justification would then rest partly on our own works.

God justifies the ungodly on the basis of Christ's work. By the sanctification of the Spirit, God makes the ungodly godly and the disobedient obedient. Therefore Paul says

---

3   Quoted by James M. Boice in *Romans*, vol. 1, *Justification by Faith (Romans 1–4)*, (Grand Rapids: Baker, 1991), 384.

4   Ibid., 383.

we *"are justified freely by his grace"* (v. 24). He uses a present passive participle, meaning we are not justifying ourselves; we are justified through the actions of another. God the Father declares us righteous in Jesus Christ.

The Source of Justification: Grace

The source of our justification is the grace of God. Paul says we are *"justified freely by his grace through the redemption that came by Christ Jesus"* (v. 24). Paul already proved that there is no one who is righteous, that all have sinned, and that the wages of sin is death. We are totally depraved and completely powerless. By grace alone can we be justified, and this grace comes to us as a gift.

Grace costs us nothing, yet it is very costly. Because God did not spare his own Son from judgment, we are spared. Think of Abraham's joy when God provided a ram in Isaac's place, and Isaac could go home with his father (Gen. 22). That ram is Jesus Christ. Grace cost the Father the death of his Son, who cried out from the cross, "My God, my God, why hast thou forsaken me?" This high cost magnifies God's grace. Away with all cheap grace! Only the costly grace of God can justify us.

God's grace gives justification to those who merited condemnation, heaven to those who merited hell, and eternal life to those who merited everlasting death. This abounding grace is greater than all our sins. Paul writes, "For if, by the trespass of the one man, death reigned through that one man, how much more will those who receive God's abundant provision of grace and of the gift of righteousness reign in life through the one man, Jesus Christ. . . . The law was added so that the trespass might increase. But where sin increased, grace increased all the more" (Rom. 5:17, 20).

This grace makes us able and more than able to do what God wants us to do. Paul says, "And God is able to make all grace abound to you, so that in all things at all times, having all that you need, you will abound in every good work" (2 Cor. 9:8). Additionally, this grace causes us to rejoice. In Greek, the word "grace" speaks about that which gives us great joy.

Although grace is a very costly gift, as we said, it costs us nothing. And because we cannot buy grace, salvation is free. Only those who have no merit of their own can receive it. So the Lord invites us: "Come, all you who are thirsty, come to the waters; and you who have no money, come, buy and eat! Come, buy wine and milk without money and without cost" (Isa. 55:1). We receive grace for nothing, yet it is the most expensive gift we can possess.

John speaks of this costly gift of grace: "[The risen Lord] said to me: 'It is done. I am the Alpha and the Omega, the Beginning and the End. To him who is thirsty I will give to drink without cost from the spring of the water of life'" (Rev. 21:6).

Again, John says, "The Spirit and the bride say, 'Come!' And let him who hears say, 'Come!' Whoever is thirsty, let him come; and whoever wishes, let him take the free gift of the water of life" (Rev. 22:17). Those who are thirsty must acknowledge they are sinners who cannot be saved without God helping them. They see their need, as did the psalmist, who declared, "As the deer pants for streams of water, so my soul pants for you, O God. My soul thirsts for God, for the living God. When can I go and meet with God?" (Ps. 42:1–2).

Jesus spoke of a king who prepared a great feast (Matt. 22:1–14). The guests were asked to come, but they all refused, saying, "I have no need of this feast. I have bought land," or "I have bought oxen," or "I am married." So the king brought in the poor, the crippled, and the blind to enjoy the feast. God's abounding grace that makes us competent is not for the rich, famous, and arrogant, but for the poor, crippled, and blind. Great salvation is for each prostitute and publican who cries out, "Have mercy on me, the sinner." Great salvation is for the thief on the cross who with his last breath entreated Jesus, "Remember me when you come into your kingdom." To such people God opens the gates of paradise and they shall feast with Christ, both now and forever.

There is no grace for proud Herods, Pilates, high priests, Pharisees, and Sadducees. Jesus saves only sinners by his amazing and abounding grace. John Stott says, "Grace is God loving, God stooping, God coming to the rescue, God giving himself generously in and through Jesus Christ."[5]

The Ground of Justification

The ground of our justification is the work of Christ—his life, death, and resurrection. Justification is not amnesty, which is pardon without principle. It is not seeing bad people as good people. Justification is based on God's justice demonstrated in the life and death of Christ. The wrath of God against elect sinners was poured out on God's innocent Son, the spotless Lamb of God. Without the cross, the justification of the unjust would be unjustified, immoral, and impossible. But Christ died for and in place of the wicked.

Paul earlier says the wrath of God is revealed against all the ungodly (Rom. 1:18). Yet he later writes, "When we were still powerless, Christ died for the ungodly" (Rom. 5:6). Therefore, we can now understand the statement in Romans 4:5: "God . . . justifies the ungodly." God does so because Christ died for the ungodly.

Jesus died as our substitute. He is our Passover Lamb. John the Baptist declared, "Look, the Lamb of God, who takes away the sin of the world!" (John 1:29). In Hebrews 9:14 we

---

5   Stott, *Romans: God's Good News*, 112.

read, "How much more, then, will the blood of Christ, who through the eternal Spirit offered himself unblemished to God, cleanse our consciences from acts that lead to death, so that we may serve the living God!"

Peter writes, "For you know that it was not with perishable things such as silver or gold that you were redeemed from the empty way of life handed down to you from your forefathers, but with the precious blood of Christ, a lamb without blemish or defect. . . . For Christ died for sins once for all, the righteous for the unrighteous, to bring you to God" (1 Pet. 1:18–19; 3:18). In our behalf Jesus satisfied the demands of all God's holy laws.

When God justifies us freely by his grace, he forgives all our sins. That is why Paul could say, "Blessed is the man whose sin the Lord will never count against him" (Rom. 4:8). Our sins are counted against Jesus Christ.

He also gives us the free gift of the righteousness of God, even the righteousness of Christ. Paul says, "For just as through the disobedience of the one man the many were made sinners, so also through the obedience of the one man the many will be made righteous" (Rom. 5:19). No longer are we under God's wrath and sin's dominion. No longer is Satan our master.

We are now under God's blessing, which justification brings to us. On the basis of Christ's substitutionary work in our behalf, we are righteous and have righteousness; we have forgiveness, eternal life, and glory; we have peace with God and experience the peace of God. As adopted children of God, we are united with Christ. All he has is ours. We have fellowship with the Father and the Son.

Paul writes of this double transaction: "God was reconciling the world to himself in Christ, not counting men's sins against them. . . . God made him who had no sin to be sin for us, so that in him we might become the righteousness of God" (2 Cor. 5:19, 21). All our sins were taken from our head and put upon Jesus, who knew no sin. Our sin became his and he atoned for it, and his righteousness is now ours.

Elsewhere Paul says, "It is because of him that you are in Christ Jesus, who has become for us wisdom from God—that is, our righteousness, holiness and redemption" (1 Cor. 1:30). Christ is our righteousness, sanctification, and redemption. Christ is not divided. If we are justified, we will be sanctified and glorified.

No longer do we try to hide under our filthy rags of self-righteousness, nor do we boast of the dung of our human merit. Covered by the blood of Christ, we are now righteous and the righteousness of God. We are in Christ. The divine judgment was hanging over us, ready to fall and execute us. But, thank God, it fell not on us, but on the One on the cross of Calvary. Now this righteousness of God has been made manifest. May we look to him and be saved!

Application Questions

1) What does justification mean? How does it relate to salvation?

2) How can a sinner like you be declared not guilty if God is perfectly just?

3) In light of this great truth, what must we conclude about our self-righteousness?

3

Redemption in Christ

²¹But now a righteousness from God, apart from law, has been made known, to which the Law and the Prophets testify. ²²This righteousness from God comes through faith in Jesus Christ to all who believe. There is no difference, ²³for all have sinned and fall short of the glory of God, ²⁴and are justified freely by his grace through the redemption that came by Christ Jesus. ²⁵God presented him as a sacrifice of atonement, through faith in his blood. He did this to demonstrate his justice, because in his forbearance he had left the sins committed beforehand unpunished— ²⁶he did it to demonstrate his justice at the present time, so as to be just and the one who justifies those who have faith in Jesus.

Romans 3:21–26

There are three sides to the triangle of salvation, described in three theological terms: justification, redemption, and propitiation. Paul speaks of being *"justified freely by his grace through the redemption that came by Christ Jesus"* (v. 24). In the last chapter, we looked at justification. In this study we will examine redemption, the second side of this triangle.

The Vocabulary of Redemption

When we study the words associated with redemption (redeem, redeemer, ransom), we find that many of them are constructed on the Greek verbal stem *lu*, which means "to loose, to set free, to liberate, to deliver from bondage to freedom." Thus we have *apoluō*, which means "to set free." Simeon used this word in reference to himself in Luke 2:29: "Sovereign Lord, as you have promised, you now *dismiss* your servant in peace." The word *lutroō* means "to set at liberty upon payment of a ransom." *Lutron* means "a ransom, the payment one makes to set someone free." *Lutrōsis* means "redemption" (see Luke 1:68). *Apolutrōsis*, which appears in Romans 3:24, means "to set a slave free upon payment of ransom, away from his former wretched condition and situation to a new situation, to a new owner, to new freedom." *Lutrōtēs*, used in reference to Moses in Acts 7:35, means "deliverer, redeemer."

Other words speak about redemption from the agora, the Greek marketplace. So we have *agorazō*, which means "to buy someone or something for oneself from the marketplace" (see 1 Cor. 6:19–20) and *exagorazō*, which means "to buy out of the marketplace, never to return to the former condition again" (see Gal. 3:13).

Slaves, prisoners of war, and captives condemned to death could be set free by another paying a ransom for them. Redemption, therefore, is releasing someone from the bondage of an alien power by paying a ransom. This ransom has to be paid by another because the captive is powerless to secure his own liberty. Captives condemned to die will surely die unless they are redeemed by another through a ransom payment.

The Scripture says we are redeemed by Jesus Christ from the alien power of Satan, from captivity to sin, from the curse of the law, from the guilt and power of sin, and from death eternal. We are redeemed to belong to our Redeemer, Jesus Christ, never again to return to our former owner and miserable situation.

Christ's redemption of us is not temporal but eternal. Speaking of the excellency and beauty of these words "redeemer" and "redemption," Everett F. Harrison declares, "No word in the Christian vocabulary deserves to be held more precious than Redeemer, for even more than Saviour it reminds the child of God that his salvation has been purchased at a great and personal cost, for the Lord has given himself for our sins in order to deliver us from them."[1]

B. B. Warfield says that Redeemer "is the name specifically of the Christ of the cross. Whenever we pronounce it, the cross is placarded before our eyes and our hearts are filled with loving remembrance not only that Christ has given us salvation but that he paid a mighty price for it."[2] Jesus himself stated, "The Son of Man did not come to be served, but to serve, and to give his life as a ransom for many" (Matt. 20:28).

Our Inability to Redeem Ourselves

Can a man redeem himself? The Bible clearly says no. The psalmist declares, "No man can redeem the life of another or give to God a ransom for him—the ransom for a life is costly, no payment is ever enough—that he should live on forever and not see decay" (Ps. 49:7–9). We read elsewhere, "If you, O Lord, kept a record of sins, O Lord, who could stand? . . . [The Lord] himself will redeem Israel from all their sins" (Ps. 130:3, 8).

Those who are not born again are in bondage to sin. "To the Jews who had believed him, Jesus said, 'If you hold to my teaching, you are really my disciples. Then

---

1   Everett F. Harrison, Geoffrey W. Bromiley, and Carl F. H. Henry, eds., *Baker's Dictionary of Theology* (Grand Rapids: Baker Book House, 1982), 439.

2   Quoted by Boice, *Romans*, vol. 1, *Justification by Faith*, 363.

you will know the truth, and the truth will set you free.' They answered him, 'We are Abraham's descendants and have never been slaves of anyone. How can you say that we shall be set free?' Jesus replied, 'I tell you the truth, everyone who sins is a slave to sin. Now a slave has no permanent place in the family, but a son belongs to it forever. So if the Son sets you free, you will be free indeed'" (John 8:31–36).

Paul makes the charge that "Jews and Gentiles alike are all under sin" (Rom. 3:9). By nature we are under the authority of master Sin and cannot free ourselves. Then Paul asserts, "*All have sinned and fall short of the glory of God*" (v. 23). Sin is the master of everyone not redeemed by Jesus Christ. Paul also comments, "We know that the law is spiritual; but I am unspiritual, sold as a slave to sin" (Rom. 7:14).

Moreover, "The wages of sin is death" (Rom. 6:23), and "The soul who sins is the one who will die" (Ezek. 18:20). We cannot get out of sin by ourselves. This is what we call total depravity.

We Need a Redeemer

We need a redeemer to set us free by payment of a ransom. In the Old Testament close relatives had certain rights: they could avenge the murder of a family member or buy back for the family any property that was sold to pay a debt. They also had the right to redeem with a ransom any family member who had sold himself as a slave or one who was under the sentence of death where such redemption was possible.[3]

---

3   For example, Exodus 21 speaks about an ox that was in the habit of goring. If the owner did not take care of it, and the ox gored and killed someone, the ox must be killed. The owner also must be killed unless someone wanted to redeem him by paying whatever price was asked.

Close relatives also had the right to marry the widows of their brothers so that the name of the dead brother would continue through the first son of the new marriage. Such a person is called a *gō'ēl*, a kinsman-redeemer. The book of Ruth is a beautiful love story that dramatizes the gracious redemption that Boaz, as kinsman-redeemer, accomplishes in buying up the property of his relative Elimelech and marrying Ruth, through whom came Christ, our great Redeemer.

We need a *gō'ēl*, a very close relative, to redeem us miserable sinners who are slaves to sin, Satan, and death. Not only must this person have the ability to pay our ransom, but he must also be willing to do so. Praise God, we have such a relative: our Lord Jesus Christ. Now we can understand more fully the importance of the incarnation of Christ.

Why did the Son of God become man? The writer to the Hebrews says, "In bringing many sons to glory, it was fitting that God, for whom and through whom everything exists, should make the author of their salvation perfect through suffering. . . . Since the children have flesh and blood, he too shared in their humanity so that by his death he might destroy him who holds the power of death—that is, the devil—and free those who all their lives were held in slavery by their fear of death" (Heb. 2:10, 14–15).

We have a close relative in Jesus Christ, and he alone is able to pay the ransom to secure our freedom because he is God-man, the sinless One. Paul writes, "[Christ Jesus], being in very nature God, did not consider equality with God something to be grasped, but made himself nothing, taking the very nature of a servant, being made in human likeness. And being found in appearance as a man, he humbled himself and became obedient to death—even death on a cross!" (Phil. 2:6–8). God became incarnate as a servant to die the shameful death of the cross so that we might be redeemed.

But is Jesus willing to redeem us? Consider the account of a leper: "When [Jesus] came down from the mountainside, large crowds followed him. A man with leprosy came and knelt before him and said, 'Lord, if you are willing, you can make me clean.' Jesus reached out his hand and touched the man. 'I am willing,' he said. 'Be clean!'" (Matt. 8:1–3). How much more willing is Jesus to redeem us from our slavery to sin!

The Old Testament speaks much of such a redeemer. In the midst of his suffering, Job declared, "I know that my Redeemer lives, and that in the end he will stand upon the earth" (Job 19:25). This was fulfilled in Jesus Christ: "The Word became flesh and made his dwelling among us. We have seen his glory, the glory of the One and Only, who came from the Father, full of grace and truth" (John 1:14).

Isaiah also spoke much about this great Redeemer's coming: "Sing for joy, O heavens, for the LORD has done this; shout aloud, O earth beneath. Burst into song, you mountains, you forests and all your trees, for the LORD has redeemed Jacob, he displays his glory in Israel" (Isa. 44:23); "Leave Babylon, flee from the Babylonians! Announce this with shouts of joy and proclaim it. Send it out to the ends of the earth; say, 'The LORD has redeemed his servant Jacob'" (Isa. 48:20); "This is what the LORD says—the Redeemer and Holy One of Israel" (Isa. 49:7); "Burst into songs of joy together, you ruins of Jerusalem, for the LORD has comforted his people, he has redeemed Jerusalem" (Isa. 52:9).

Who Is the Promised Redeemer?

This redeemer promised in the Old Testament is none other than Jesus Christ. He is our *gō'ēl*, our kinsman-redeemer. The angel told Joseph, "You are to give him the name Jesus, because he will save his people from their sins" (Matt. 1:21). Zechariah prophesied about the redemption Christ would bring: "Praise be to the Lord, the God of Israel, because he has come and has redeemed his people" (Luke 1:68). Anna spoke similarly to the parents of the infant Jesus: "Coming up to them at that very moment, she gave thanks to God and spoke about the child to all who were looking forward to the redemption of Jerusalem" (Luke 2:38).

Paul remarks, "In him we have redemption through his blood, the forgiveness of sins" (Eph. 1:7). Elsewhere he writes, "For he has rescued us from the dominion of darkness and brought us into the kingdom of the Son he loves, in whom we have redemption, the forgiveness of sins" (Col. 1:13–14).

In Hebrews 7:22, Jesus is called our "sponsor," which means he is responsible for all our obligations. Jesus guarantees our total and final salvation because of his person and permanent priesthood. There is no redemption outside of the person of Jesus Christ. There is no salvation in any other name. Jesus Christ alone is our Redeemer.

The High Cost of Redemption

Not only is Jesus our Redeemer, but he is also the ransom price paid for our redemption. All creation came into being by a command of God, but redemption was achieved by the incarnation and death of God's Son. This great price shows how much God loves us.

Paul spoke of this high cost of redemption to the Ephesian elders: "Keep watch over yourselves and all the flock of which the Holy Spirit has made you overseers. Be shepherds of the church of God, which he bought with his own blood" (Acts 20:28). Jesus himself spoke of this price: "I am the good shepherd. The good shepherd lays down his life for the sheep" (John 10:11).

Peter declares, "For you know that it was not with perishable things such as silver or gold that you were redeemed from the empty way of life handed down to you from your forefathers, but with the precious blood of Christ, a lamb without blemish or defect" (1 Pet. 1:18–19). We see the same idea in 1 Corinthians 6:19–20: "Do you not know that your body is a temple of the Holy Spirit, who is in you, whom you have received from God? You are not your own; you were bought at a price. Therefore honor God with your body."

The Hebrews writer tells us, "Without the shedding of blood there is no forgiveness" (Heb. 9:22). The blood of bulls and goats cannot forgive our sins. Only the blood of God's Son can redeem us. But Jesus did not give his life to ransom every sinner. Jesus died to redeem only his elect sinners whose names are written in the Lamb's book of life.

So Paul writes, "For he chose us in him before the creation of the world to be holy and blameless in his sight" (Eph. 1:4). If everyone was chosen, then choosing would have no meaning. In his high priestly prayer, Jesus says of his disciples, "I pray for them. I am not praying for the world, but for those you have given me, for they are yours" (John 17:9). There is a distinction. The church is an inner circle; the outer circle is the world. We are the Father's donation to the Son, that he may redeem us at the high price of his own death.

Jesus said to the unbelieving Jews, "You do not believe me because you are not my sheep. My sheep listen to my voice; I know them, and they follow me. I give them eternal life, and they shall never perish; no one can snatch them out of my hand" (John 10:26–28). J. I. Packer says, "The death of Christ actually put away the sins of all God's elect and ensured that they would be brought to faith through regeneration and kept in faith for glory."[4]

---

4   J. I. Packer, *Concise Theology* (Wheaton, IL: Tyndale House Publishers, 1993), 137.

There are three views of how many people Christ died for. First, there is actual universalism, which says Christ died for everyone without exception, so everyone without exception will be saved. Adherents of this view say the death of Christ has unlimited extent and unlimited efficacy. Second, there is hypothetical universalism, which says Christ's death has unlimited extent but limited efficacy. Third, there is particular redemption, which says Christ's death has unlimited efficacy but limited extent— limited to the salvation of God's elect. We agree with this last view: Jesus Christ died for everyone who will repent and believe in him.

Present and Future Redemption

We experience the blessing of God's redemption in two stages. The first stage is the present time, and the second stage is in the coming age. Paul writes, "In him we have redemption through his blood, the forgiveness of sins" (Eph. 1:7). We presently experience forgiveness of all our sins. That is what it means to be justified. Paul says elsewhere: "For he has rescued us from the dominion of darkness and brought us into the kingdom of the Son he loves, in whom we have redemption, the forgiveness of sins" (Col. 1:13–14). Even now we are experiencing the kingdom of God, which is "righteousness, peace and joy in the Holy Spirit" (Rom. 14:17).

Paul writes that Jesus "gave himself for us to redeem us from all wickedness [lawlessness] and to purify for himself a people that are his very own, eager to do what is good" (Titus 2:14). What a blessing it is to be redeemed from lawlessness! We find the same word for lawlessness (*anomia*) in Matthew 7, where Jesus says many will come to him, saying, "Lord, Lord." And he will tell them, "Depart from me, you workers of lawlessness" (Matt. 7:22–23, author's translation). The problem of many evangelical churches today is that they speak of justification but practice lawlessness. But God has redeemed us from all lawlessness and is purifying us to be his own holy people, zealous to do what is good.

In 1 Corinthians 6:18–20, Paul exhorts us to flee from sexual immorality. Some modern evangelicals not only say we do not have to flee sexual immorality, but also teach that Christians can indulge in it and still be saved! But that is not what the Bible teaches. "Flee from sexual immorality. All other sins a man commits are outside his body, but he who sins sexually sins against his own body. Do you not know that your body is a temple of the Holy Spirit, who is in you, whom you have received from God?"

The Holy Spirit is in us; this is a present blessing. Paul continues, "You are not your own; you were bought at a price." Many who sinned against their bodies have lived to regret it. True Christians will not boast of how much immorality they committed; rather, they will be ashamed, because sin is injurious to both body and soul. But now our ownership has been changed from Satan to Jesus Christ. Paul concludes, "Therefore honor God with your body." These are all present experiences of redemption.

What is going to happen in the future? Paul writes, "We know that the whole creation has been groaning as in the pains of childbirth right up to the present time. Not only so, but we ourselves, who have the firstfruits of the Spirit, groan inwardly as we wait eagerly for our adoption as sons, the redemption of our bodies" (Rom. 8:22–23). In our future installment of redemption, we will receive a glorified, sinless, Spirit-engineered physical body with which to live with God.

We are all going to die. God has decided to give us the fullness of the blessings of redemption in two installments. We may want it in one, but that is not God's plan. So we must die, but we will die in faith and in the sure hope that we will be with Christ in paradise.

Paul writes, "And you also were included in Christ when you heard the word of truth, the gospel of your salvation. Having believed, you were marked in him with a seal, the promised Holy Spirit" (Eph. 1:13). The Holy Spirit is the seal that signifies, first, ownership, that we belong to Christ; and, second, security, that we are secure in Christ. The Holy Spirit "is a deposit guaranteeing our inheritance until the redemption of those who are God's possession—to the praise of his glory" (Eph. 1:14). Here redemption is seen as future: Paul is speaking about the glorification of our bodies. In the same epistle he says, "Do not grieve the Holy Spirit of God, with whom you were sealed for the day of redemption" (Eph. 4:30).

The Blessings of Redemption

What blessings do we receive from this aspect of salvation called redemption?

1. *We enjoy freedom.* "It is for freedom that Christ has set us free. Stand firm, then, and do not let yourselves be burdened again by a yoke of slavery" (Gal. 5:1). As redeemed people of God, we enjoy freedom from sin, guilt, condemnation, death, and hell. We enjoy freedom to say no to sin and yes to righteousness. What glorious freedom— we do not have to sin! When Jesus was tempted, he said no to sin and yes to God. We have the same freedom.

How many people in today's churches think that because they are justified, they can do whatever they want! Such people say that repentance is not necessary and that Christians do not have to produce even one fruit of the Spirit. But Paul says, "You, my brothers, were called to be free. But do not use your freedom to indulge the sinful nature; rather, serve one another in love" (Gal. 5:13).

Jesus said, "I tell you the truth, everyone who sins is a slave to sin. Now a slave has no permanent place in the family, but a son belongs to it forever. So if the Son sets you free, you will be free indeed" (John 8:34–36). If we are sons of God, we must stand fast in the freedom Christ has given us.

2. *We have a new master.* In Ephesians 1:13–14 Paul writes that we are sealed with the Holy Spirit, demonstrating that we belong to our new master, Jesus Christ, to serve and love him. This change of ownership is what makes us Christians: "If you confess with your mouth, 'Jesus is Lord,' and believe in your heart that God raised him from the dead, you will be saved" (Rom. 10:9).

Jesus tells us, "Come to me, all you who are weary and burdened, and I will give you rest. Take my yoke upon you and learn from me, for I am gentle and humble in heart, and you will find rest for your souls. For my yoke is easy and my burden is light" (Matt. 11:28–30). Christianity is an ongoing relational life with our new master, Jesus. There is no such thing as absolute freedom. All people serve either Satan or Christ.

3. *We experience forgiveness of all sins.* "In him we have redemption through his blood, the forgiveness of sins" (Eph. 1:7).

4. *We enjoy the redemption of our bodies.* Jesus was sent to bring many sons to glory, and God will glorify us in body and soul, saving us not only from the penalty and power of sin but also from the presence of sin. Today sin is present in us, but there is coming a day when our bodies will be like unto Christ's glorious body. "We shall be like him, for we shall see him as he is" (1 John 3:2).

5. *Sin has no dominion over us.* This may sound strange to us, but it is true, even in this life. Paul writes, "For sin shall not be your master" (Rom. 6:14). Our new master is the Lord Jesus Christ; we need no longer obey sin.

6. *We are not under law.* "But when the time had fully come, God sent his Son, born of a woman, born under law, to redeem those under law" (Gal. 4:4–5). We can now stand before God, not because we kept the law perfectly

but because Jesus Christ did. We are not under law but under grace. This grace enables us to fulfill the law: to love our spouses, to go to work, to tell the truth, to stop stealing and work with our hands that we may have something to give, to honor our father and mother.

God's moral laws are still applicable to us, but we as sinners can never keep them perfectly and stand before God in our own righteousness. Paul says, "In the same way, count yourselves dead to sin but alive to God in Christ Jesus" (Rom. 6:11). In his great love and rich mercy, God made us alive that we might serve him. This is spiritual resurrection. In our souls we possess the life of God, by which we can resist the devil and enjoy the freedom to say no to sin. What we read about in Ephesians 2:1–3 has been reversed. Now we are alive toward God and dead toward sin—not dead *in* sin, but *toward* sin.

7. *Satan cannot harm us.* John admonishes, "We know that anyone born of God does not continue to sin; the one who was born of God keeps him safe, and the evil one cannot harm him" (1 John 5:18). Jesus declares, "I give them eternal life, and they shall never perish; no one can snatch them out of my hand" (John 10:28). Satan can never harm God's people. James exhorts, "Resist the devil, and he will flee from you" (James 4:7). The devil is a superhuman, angelic being. Yet we can resist him in the name of Jesus Christ and he will run.

Peter speaks of this: "Your enemy the devil prowls around like a roaring lion looking for someone to devour. Resist him, standing firm in the faith" (1 Pet. 5:8–9). We do not have to sin. We sin because we are arrogant, and pride goes before a fall. If you are not listening when the word is preached, be careful. You may soon fall. The devil's purpose is to keep us from God's word because it is the divine medicine that will heal us if we take it. Those who are humble, who listen to and fear God, can resist the devil in the name of Jesus by obeying Christ. That is what standing firm in the faith means. When we do so, he will flee. John writes, "They overcame [the devil] by the blood of the Lamb and by the word of their testimony" (Rev. 12:11).

8. *Redemption brings sonship.* "But when the time had fully come, God sent his Son, born of a woman, born under law, to redeem those under law, that we might receive the full rights of sons" (Gal. 4:4–5). We now belong to the family of God, and our status brings us inheritance. As sons, we are heirs of God and joint-heirs with Christ.

Sonship also brings the Spirit of God's Son into our hearts. How do we know that the Holy Spirit is in us? We will have a continuous cry: "*Abba,* Father." Children cry when they are born. In fact, we look for that cry as a sign of life; otherwise, it may be a stillbirth. We are to cry out continuously to our heavenly Father. It is automatic for a redeemed child of God to do so. We have been brought into the family of God and given the right of sons to cry out to our Father, who promises to hear us.

I pray that each of us will make certain that we belong to the company of the redeemed. When God saves us, he delivers us from all bondages and brings us into the glorious liberty of the children of God. Make sure, therefore, that you belong to Jesus Christ, the Redeemer, who loved us so much he laid down his own life for our redemption—a redemption that is just as irreversible and irrevocable as justification. And having been redeemed out of our former sphere of sin, guilt, and misery, we now belong to the family of God. We now can enjoy a life of freedom—freedom not to sin and freedom to obey God.

Application Questions

1) What does redemption mean? How does it relate to salvation?

2) Why is Jesus Christ the only one capable of redeeming us from our sins?

3) What did Jesus do to accomplish our redemption?

4

Salvation
as Propitiation

[21] But now a righteousness from God, apart from law, has been made known, to which the Law and the Prophets testify. [22] This righteousness from God comes through faith in Jesus Christ to all who believe. There is no difference, [23] for all have sinned and fall short of the glory of God, [24] and are justified freely by his grace through the redemption that came by Christ Jesus. [25] God presented him as a sacrifice of atonement, through faith in his blood. He did this to demonstrate his justice, because in his forbearance he had left the sins committed beforehand unpunished— [26] he did it to demonstrate his justice at the present time, so as to be just and the one who justifies those who have faith in Jesus.

Romans 3:21–26

In Romans 3:21–26, salvation is seen from three perspectives: justification, redemption, and propitiation. The last doctrine, propitiation, speaks about the Christ of the cross. It is a forgotten doctrine greatly detested by theological liberals who do not believe in the authority of the Bible, the deity of Christ, miracles, heaven and hell, or the fall of man.

41

Liberal versions of the Bible translate the Greek word *hilasterion* in Romans 3:25 as "expiation" instead of "propitiation." But "propitiation" is correctly used by the King James Version, the English Standard Version, and the New American Standard Version. First, then, we must explore the meaning of this word propitiation.

Definition of Propitiation

Propitiation has to do with offering a sacrifice to appease an angry God so that he may be favorably disposed, or propitious, to the one making an offering. In contrast, expiation has no Godward reference. It speaks about cancellation of sins, but only in reference to man. In other words, expiation eliminates a God who is angry against human sin.

The word "propitiation" is taken from the world of ancient religion, just as justification comes from the legal world, and redemption comes from the marketplace. We see illustrations of propitiation in the religious world even today. Years ago, I visited a country where people would leave offerings such as flowers, food, cigarettes, and other commodities for their gods. These worshipers were trying to appease the wrath of their gods so that they in turn would be gracious to them.

In many churches today, the God of the Bible is not seen as angry or wrathful, but as an indulgent grandfather, a jolly Santa Claus who approves everything we do. Propitiation is not necessary with such a God. Additionally, liberal theologians have declared that propitiation is not a biblical idea. But the Bible speaks of a wrathful God on nearly every page.

In the Old Testament, there are twenty different Hebrew words used some 580 times to express God's wrath against the sin of his people. And in Romans 1:18–3:20, Paul speaks clearly of the wrath of God being revealed against all ungodliness and unrighteousness of men. He concludes that passage stating that all have sinned against God's law and are under his wrath.

When Paul speaks of propitiation, he is not speaking of the capricious wrath of pagan deities; he is speaking of the stern and settled reaction of the holy God against the evil of man. Leon Morris states: "Certainly we must retain the idea of the wrath of God, for, as Edwyn Bevan has pointed out, the idea that God cannot be angry is neither Hebrew nor Christian, but something borrowed from Greek philosophy."[1]

Ancient Greek philosophers spoke of a god who was without feelings and therefore could not become angry. But such an apathetic God also cannot be loving. Theological liberals who speak about a non-wrathful God who is love and always forgives fail to deduce that if God is not wrathful, his love and forgiveness are meaningless.

The Scriptures teach about the wrath of God because it highlights the seriousness of sin. God hates sin with a perfect hatred (Ps. 11:5). Jesus himself often spoke of the eternal, unquenchable fires of hell. The writer to the Hebrews speaks about God as a consuming fire (Heb. 12:29). It is only through God's own propitiation that his wrath can be averted and we can be brought into a new relationship with him.

Seeing how God's people were destroyed by the Babylonians, Jeremiah wrote, "We have sinned and rebelled and you have not forgiven. You have covered yourself with anger and pursued us; you have slain without pity. You have covered yourself with a cloud so that no prayer can get through. You have made us scum and refuse among the nations. All our enemies have opened their mouths wide against us" (Lam. 3:42–46). The entire book of Lamentations reveals a God who was angry with his people.

---

1   Leon Morris, *The Apostolic Preaching of the Cross* (Grand Rapids: Eerdmans, 1965), 212.

The psalmist says, "You are not a God who takes pleasure in evil; with you the wicked cannot dwell. The arrogant cannot stand in your presence; you hate all who do wrong. You destroy those who tell lies; bloodthirsty and deceitful men the LORD abhors" (Ps. 5:4–6).

Jesus can also become angry (Mark 3:5). John speaks of the wrath of the Lamb (Rev. 6:16; 19:15; see also 2 Thess. 1:7–9). Therefore, we do not believe in an apathetic god of Greek philosophy, who neither becomes angry nor loves. We believe in the holy God of the Scriptures, who hates sin and punishes sinners.

Then we must ask: If God hates sin and punishes sinners, and all men are under God's wrath because all have sinned, how can anyone be saved from God's wrath? The answer is found in this passage: *"There is no difference, for all have sinned and fall short of the glory of God, and are justified freely by his grace through the redemption which is in Christ Jesus, whom God displayed publicly as a propitiation [a sacrifice of atonement] through faith in his blood"* (vv. 23–25, author's translation).

God Initiated Propitiation

Sinful man did not come up with a sacrifice to appease God's wrath. God himself took the initiative to provide us with a sufficient propitiation to deal with all our sins. In pagan religions, man brings an offering to appease the wrath of his god, but in Christianity man is not propitiating God.

In one sense, it is not even Jesus Christ who propitiates God's wrath. God the Father took the initiative according to his own predeterminate counsel to appease his own wrath that he may be gracious to us and forgive our sins. Jehovah Jireh, the God who provides, especially provides for our salvation. So Paul writes, *"God presented him as propitiation"* (v. 25), or *"whom God publicly displayed as propitiation.*" In this God-initiated propitiation, God's holy wrath and his love for sinners meet on the cross. God is holy; therefore, he must punish sinners. Yet God is also love and does not want to punish sinners. Thus, he punished a substitute in our stead—his own sinless Son. The entire Old Testament pointed to this substitutionary propitiation in the sacrificial system.

In Leviticus 17:11 we read, "For the life of a creature is in the blood, and I have given it to you to make atonement for yourselves on the altar; it is the blood that makes atonement for one's life." John writes, "For God so loved the world that he gave his one and only Son" (John 3:16). God gave his Son in sacrificial death to make atonement for our sins.

Paul says, "He was delivered over to death for our sins and was raised to life for our justification." He later affirms, "But God demonstrates his own love for us in this: While we were still sinners, Christ died for us" (Rom. 4:25; 5:8). John declares, "This is love: not that we loved God, but that he loved us and sent his Son as propitiation for our sins" (1 John 4:10, author's translation). The NIV translates *hilasmos* as "an atoning sacrifice" for our sins.

God Publicly Displayed His Son

On the cross, God presented his Son as propitiation (Rom. 3:25). He put him forward, exhibiting him before the entire world to look at and ask why this innocent Son of God was being crucified. Paul writes of this public declaration: *"But now a righteousness from God, apart from law, has been made known"* (v. 21). This is speaking about the cross on Calvary's hill.

Because of the sinful murmuring of his people in the desert, God sent poisonous serpents to bite them (see Numbers 21). After many people died, the rest acknowledged their sin. Then God instructed Moses to make a brazen serpent and lift it up so that all who looked at it would be healed.

Jesus Christ spoke often of this idea in connection with his own crucifixion: "Just as Moses lifted up the snake in the desert, so the Son of Man must be lifted up" (John 3:14); "When you have lifted up the Son of Man, then you will know that I am the one that I claim to be, and that I do nothing on my own but speak just what the Father has taught me" (John 8:28); "But I, when I am lifted up from the earth, will draw all men to myself" (John 12:32).

Christ was displayed publicly in the midst of the universe in time and space on Calvary's hill for all intelligent beings, both human and angelic, to consider and ask why. Think about this action God the Father took. All people of the world must think about the crucified Christ. Peter tells us, "This man was handed over to you by God's set purpose and foreknowledge" (Acts 2:23). God delivered his Son over and publicly displayed him on the cross for his own glory, that his righteousness be displayed in this exhibition. God is declaring that he hates and punishes sin instead of passing over it.

God was glorified when he punished our sin in his Son. This was also the Son's prayer: "'Now my heart is troubled, and what shall I say? "Father, save me from this hour"? No, it was for this very reason I came to this hour. Father, glorify your name!' Then a voice came from heaven, 'I have glorified it, and will glorify it again'" (John 12:27–28).

The public display of God's Son on the cross brings glory to God's name. The Father displayed him for the world as a sacrifice of atonement. Unless a God-given sinless substitute dies in our stead, we must die, for we must suffer the fullness of God's wrath against our sin. The whole sacrificial system, therefore, teaches propitiation: the removal of God's wrath by a sacrifice so that God may be propitious to us, forgive all our sins, and restore us to favor and fellowship. "Without the shedding of blood there is no forgiveness" (Heb. 9:22). But whose blood is to be shed? Whose death ensures the appeasing of God's wrath?

Propitiation through the Blood of the Lamb

The writer to the Hebrews clearly states, "It is impossible for the blood of bulls and goats to take away sins" (Heb. 10:4). All the sacrificial animal blood that was shed throughout the Old Testament era pointed to the blood of the Lamb of God who alone can take away the sin of the world (John 1:29). The apostle writes, "[Christ] is the atoning sacrifice for our sins, and not only for ours but also for the sins of the whole world" (1 John 2:2).

Leviticus 16 describes the Day of Atonement, when sin offerings were offered for the sin of Aaron and his family, and also for the sins of all Israel. On that day, the high priest, properly washed and dressed, would go into the Holy of Holies carrying incense and the blood of the bull and goat sin offerings. He could enter this Most Holy Place only on the Day of Atonement.

Inside the Most Holy Place was an ark with a golden cover, on either end of which stood cherubim, whose wings overshadowed this golden lid, called the mercy seat. The mercy seat was the place of propitiation. It covered the ark, which contained tablets of God's commandments that man has broken. Man is guilty and God is angry, and God is seen as enthroned above this golden cover.

When the high priest came in, he sprinkled blood from the sacrificed animals on the mercy seat and in front of it. The idea was that God would look down on the blood-sprinkled cover of the ark and see the blood. The guilt of man's sin was therefore removed by the death of the God-given substitute, and the wrath of God was averted. God could now be gracious to forgive and restore man into favor and fellowship. Thus, the sins of Aaron and the people of Israel were forgiven (Lev. 16:34).

Who is the God-given substitute whose death averts God's wrath against us? Whose death removes our sins from God's sight? It is Jesus Christ, whom God publicly displayed upon the cross as our propitiation. He is our mercy seat, as well as our sinless and eternal high priest. He is the God-provided victim who offered himself on the altar of the cross to appease God's wrath against us.

Hebrews 2:14 speaks about our kinsman-redeemer, Jesus Christ, who became incarnate that he may redeem us. The word "to propitiate" is found in Hebrews 2:17: "For this reason he had to be made like his brothers in every way, in order that he might become a merciful and faithful high priest in service to God [in dealing with things pertaining to God in behalf of us], and that he might make atonement [propitiate] for the sins of the people."

And in Hebrews 2:9 we read, "But we see Jesus, who was made a little lower than the angels, now crowned with glory and honor because he suffered death, so that by the grace of God he might taste death for everyone." He is the propitiation, the sacrifice of atonement, who tasted death in behalf of us.

God presented Christ as a propitiation through faith in his blood (v. 25). Paul tells us that this propitiation was objectively achieved by Christ's blood poured out in his sacrificial death. Christ's shed blood is the means by which God's wrath is propitiated. The blood defines that in which the propitiatory sacrifice consisted, for the outpoured blood proves death has occurred. In John 10, Jesus declares five times that he will lay down his life for his sheep. In the same gospel, John describes how all the blood was drained out of this final sacrificial victim on the cross (John 19:34).

The Hebrews writer says, "Therefore, brothers, . . . we have confidence to enter the Most Holy Place by the blood of Jesus" (Heb. 10:19). Peter declares, "For you know that it was not with perishable things such as silver or gold that you were redeemed from the empty way of life handed down to you from your forefathers, but with the precious blood of Christ, a lamb without blemish or defect" (1 Pet. 1:18–19). Propitiation was achieved, not by our blood, but by the blood of the Lord Jesus Christ, our God-given substitute.

Jesus Is Our Substitute

Jesus Christ is our propitiation. Isaiah 53 tells us that he is our substitute, the Lamb of God who takes away the sin of the world. Paul writes, "For Christ's love compels us, because we are convinced that one died for all, and therefore all died. . . . God was reconciling the world to himself in Christ, not counting men's sins against them. . . . God made him who had no sin to be sin for us, so that in him we might become the righteousness of God" (2 Cor. 5:14, 19, 21).

Peter tells us, "He himself bore our sins in his body on the tree, so that we might die to sins and live for righteousness; by his wounds you have been healed. . . . For Christ died for sins once for all, the righteous for the unrighteous, to bring you to God. He was put to death in the body but made alive by the Spirit" (1 Pet. 2:24; 3:18). In Christ, the wrath of God against sinners vanishes because the wrath of God in its fullness descended on this God-given substitute who cried out from the cross, "My God, my God, why hast thou forsaken me?" (Matt. 27:46, KJV).

For many years, John Bunyan was anxious about his salvation. Then God gave him this idea: "Sinner, thou thinkest that because of thy sins and infirmities I cannot save thy soul, but behold, my Son is by me, and upon him I look, and not on thee, and will deal with thee according as I am pleased with him."[2]

---

2   John Bunyan, *Grace Abounding to the Chief of Sinners* as found in *The Works of John Bunyan*, vol. 1 (Edinburgh: Banner of Truth, 1991), 39.

Christ died in our place and for our sins; we are accepted in the Beloved. When God sees the blood of his Son, he passes over our sins because they are punished fully in him. Jesus is our Passover and propitiation.

This propitiation has four aspects: first, the offense, or the sin to be taken away; second, the offended party (God), who must be pacified and reconciled; third, the offending person, who must be pardoned and received by God; and, fourth, a sacrifice that must be offered to make atonement.

When Christ died, our sin was cancelled, God's wrath was appeased and taken away, and now we are forgiven and restored. Paul writes, "But now in Christ Jesus you who once were far away have been brought near" (Eph. 2:13). We have been brought into God's kingdom and into God's family—nearer we cannot be. We are in God and God is in us. God demanded propitiation and, thank God, he provided it.

No wonder Paul gloried in the cross! He reveled in preaching Christ as our atonement and propitiation: "We preach Christ crucified: a stumbling block to Jews and foolishness to Gentiles, but to those whom God has called, both Jews and Greeks, Christ the power of God and the wisdom of God. . . . For I resolved to know nothing while I was with you except Jesus Christ and him crucified" (1 Cor. 1:23–24; 2:2). That is why Paul rebuked the Galatians for considering abandoning their faith: "You foolish Galatians! Who has bewitched you? Before your very eyes Jesus Christ was clearly portrayed [placarded] as crucified" (Gal. 3:1). Then he declares, "May I never boast except in the cross of our Lord Jesus Christ" (Gal. 6:14).

Propitiation Proves God's Righteousness

What is the purpose of Christ's propitiation in our behalf? It proves that God is righteous and just when he justifies a wicked person who believes in Jesus. In his forbearance, God passed over sins committed by the saints of the Old Testament. In other words, he did not punish the sins of the saints of the old covenant. Yet they were fully forgiven of their sins, for they trusted in the Messiah who was to come through the God-given sacrificial system. The saints of the Old Testament looked forward to the cross and their sins were forgiven; we look backward to the cross for the forgiveness of our sins.

Because God passed over the sins committed formerly without punishing them, one could argue that God is indifferent to the claims of divine justice. For example, King David committed adultery and murdered a believer, and Leviticus 20:10 and 24:17 call for the death penalty for such sins.

But look at the language used by Nathan the prophet when David confessed his sin: "Then David said to Nathan, 'I have sinned against the LORD.' Nathan replied, 'The LORD has taken away your sin. You are not going to die'" (2 Sam. 12:13). What about God and his justice? How can God do this when his own word says to kill those like David who commit such sins? This passage in Romans tells us that God passed over the sins of God's people in the Old Testament in his forbearance because he was going to propitiate them in Christ. The cross, then, proves the righteous character of God because all the sins of the saints of the Old Testament were punished in Jesus Christ on the cross, as well as all the sins of believers who live after Christ.

We must understand that the sins of all the people of the world were not punished in Christ when he died on the cross, but only those of God's people, past, present, and future. All have sinned, and the wages of sin is death—not just physical and spiritual death, but eternal death—being eternally removed from God's presence. That is what Jesus experienced on the cross. He went to hell in our place.

Propitiation, therefore, upholds God's justice. Because God hates sin, he graciously punishes all our sin in his Son. God pronounces wicked sinners to be legally righteous because God himself, in his Son, bore the penalty for our law-breaking. Isaiah speaks about this: "But he was pierced for our transgressions, he was crushed for our iniquities; the punishment that brought us peace was upon him, and by his wounds we are healed. We all, like sheep, have gone astray, each of us has turned to his own way; and the LORD has laid on him the iniquity of us all" (Isa. 53:5–6).

Therefore, the propitiation of Christ's death on the cross proves, first, that God is righteous in his nature; second, that God punishes every sin of his elect; third, that God is just when he justifies sinners who believe in Jesus; and, fourth, that God will punish justly every sinner who refuses to trust in Jesus for every sin he committed.

Effects of Propitiation

What are the effects of this sacrifice of atonement?

1. *God forgives all our sins.* The Bible speaks of God blotting out our sins and remembering them no more, of removing them to the farthest extent of the universe, and of burying them in the very depths of the ocean. All these metaphors tell us that when God forgives our sins, he removes all our sin, guilt, death, hell, and condemnation. Imagine the joy of Isaac and his father when God told Abraham to stop sacrificing Isaac and then provided a ram to be sacrificed in the place of Isaac. What relief! What inexpressible joy of both the father and the son! We can imagine the great excitement of Abraham and Isaac as they rejoined the servants and went home to tell Sarah what had happened. That is salvation. Our sins are forgiven and our guilt is taken away.

2. *We gain access to God.* As rebellious sinners, we were far from God. But now we have access to God. What

happened at the moment Christ died? "When Jesus had cried out again in a loud voice, he gave up his spirit. At that moment the curtain of the temple was torn in two from top to bottom" (Matt. 27:50–51). There was a thick curtain that prevented not only ordinary Israelites and the priests but even the high priest from entering into the presence of God. Any who came in would experience death. Fire from the Most Holy Place would kill them, as it did Nadab and Abihu (Lev. 10).

But now the curtain has been torn by God from top to bottom, and a new way is opened up so that we can go into the very presence of God in the name of Jesus Christ. Paul writes, "Therefore, since we have been justified through faith, we have peace with God through our Lord Jesus Christ, through whom we have gained access by faith into this grace in which we now stand. And we rejoice in the hope of the glory of God" (Rom. 5:1–2).

In Ephesians 2 Paul gives us an understanding of who we were and what Christ has done for us: "Therefore, remember that formerly you who are Gentiles by birth and called 'uncircumcised' by those who call themselves 'the circumcision' (that done in the body by the hands of men)—remember that at that time you were separate from Christ, excluded from citizenship in Israel and foreigners to the covenants of the promise, without hope and without God in the world. But now in Christ Jesus you who once were far away have been brought near through the blood of Christ" (Eph. 2:11–13). All hindrances have been removed.

The writer to the Hebrews exhorts, "Therefore, brothers, since we have confidence to enter the Most Holy Place by the blood of Jesus, by a new and living way opened for us through the curtain, that is, his body, and since we have a great priest over the house of God, let us draw near to God with a sincere heart in full assurance of faith, having our hearts sprinkled to cleanse us from a guilty conscience and having our bodies washed with pure water" (Heb. 10:19–22).

Before, we did not have confidence. We were depressed because of the guilt of our sin. Our guilt was like an iron girder that sat on us and pushed us down. Our faces were downcast and we could not rejoice. But through Christ, our guilt is gone and we have confidence to come into God's presence. We can come to God to pray and enjoy the sunshine of his glorious presence.

Through the propitiatory sacrifice of Christ, we now can come to God. The Hebrews writer says, "But you have come to Mount Zion, to the heavenly Jerusalem, the city of the living God. You have come to thousands upon thousands of angels in joyful assembly, to the church of the firstborn, whose names are written in heaven. You have come to God, the judge of all men, to the spirits of righteous men made perfect, to Jesus the mediator of a new covenant, and to the sprinkled blood that speaks a better word than the blood of Abel" (Heb. 12:22–24). The better word of the blood of Christ is a word of forgiveness, grace, and acceptance. Christ's sprinkled blood is our passport to heaven.

3. *We now experience no condemnation.* Paul writes, "Therefore, there is now no condemnation for those who are in Christ Jesus" (Rom. 8:1). We are no longer condemned, because we are justified. After her accusers left, Jesus asked the woman caught in adultery: "'Woman, where are they? Has no one condemned you?' 'No one, sir,' she said. 'Then neither do I condemn you,' Jesus declared. 'Go now and leave your life of sin'" (John 8:10–11).

In Luke 18 we see a terrible sinner, a publican, coming to the temple: "But the tax collector stood at a distance. He would not even look up to heaven, but beat his breast and said, 'God, have mercy on me, a sinner'" (v. 13). In the Greek it is, "God, be propitiated with reference to me, the sinner," that is, on the basis of the sprinkled blood on the mercy seat. This publican understood something about propitiation. We read that he went home justified, while the Pharisee went home condemned.

Our Need for Propitiation

We need God's propitiation for our sins. Because we are sinners, God's wrath is resting upon us (Rom. 1:18). The wages of sin is death; therefore, we must die. Being sinners, we cannot initiate or effect propitiation ourselves. We cannot bring a chicken or a cigarette or some flowers to God and expect him to turn away his wrath and be gracious to us. As sinners, all we do is sinful; therefore, we cannot propitiate our sins. We need a substitute, a kinsman-redeemer, an advocate, a mediator who is able to propitiate in behalf of us.

God has displayed Jesus Christ publicly as our propitiation, our sacrifice of atonement, on the cross. Our job is to confess our sins and believe in the Lord Jesus Christ, and God's gracious job is to remove the guilt of our sin. When we believe on him, God's wrath disappears. We are saved and shall live forever in God's presence.

But if we do not believe in Christ, the cross demonstrates that God must punish to the fullest extent anyone who refuses to trust in Jesus. John writes, "Whoever believes in the Son has eternal life, but whoever rejects the Son will not see life, for God's wrath remains on him" (John 3:36). Those who do not trust in Christ must find their own atonement, which is impossible to do. Propitiation is found only in Jesus Christ.

This is not mythology or false threatening. John writes, "Once more Jesus said to them, 'I am going away, and you will look for me, and you will die in your sin. Where I go, you cannot come.' This made the Jews ask, 'Will he kill himself? Is that why he says, "Where I go, you cannot come"?' But he continued, 'You are from below; I am from above. You are of this world; I am not of this world. I told you that you would die in your sins; if you do not believe that I am the one I claim to be, you will indeed die in your sins'" (John 8:21–24).

God must deal with those who do not trust in his Son. Paul writes, "God is just: He will pay back trouble to those who trouble you and give relief to you who are troubled, and to us as well. This will happen when the Lord Jesus is revealed from heaven in blazing fire with his powerful angels. He will punish those who do not know God and do not obey the gospel of our Lord Jesus. They will be punished with everlasting destruction and shut out from the presence of the Lord and from the majesty of his power on the day he comes to be glorified in his holy people and to be marveled at among all those who have believed" (2 Thess. 1:6–10).

Thank God that he regenerated us and gave us the gift of repentance and faith! God enabled us to lift up our empty beggar-hands to receive this great salvation as a free gift. Christ opened up the way to the Father and now we can come with confidence and full assurance that he will receive us. Thank God for the propitiatory death of Christ on our behalf!

Application Questions

1) What does propitiation mean? How does it relate to salvation?

2) Why could only Jesus Christ be our propitiation?

3) How does this doctrine of propitiation show that God is just?

5

Sola Fide

²¹But now a righteousness from God, apart from law, has been made known, to which the Law and the Prophets testify. ²²This righteousness from God comes through faith in Jesus Christ to all who believe. There is no difference, ²³for all have sinned and fall short of the glory of God, ²⁴and are justified freely by his grace through the redemption that came by Christ Jesus. ²⁵God presented him as a sacrifice of atonement, through faith in his blood. He did this to demonstrate his justice, because in his forbearance he had left the sins committed beforehand unpunished— ²⁶he did it to demonstrate his justice at the present time, so as to be just and the one who justifies those who have faith in Jesus.

²⁷Where, then, is boasting? It is excluded. On what principle? On that of observing the law? No, but on that of faith. ²⁸For we maintain that a man is justified by faith apart from observing the law. ²⁹Is God the God of Jews only? Is he not the God of Gentiles too? Yes, of Gentiles too, ³⁰since there is only one God, who will justify the circumcised by faith and the uncircumcised through that same faith. ³¹Do we, then, nullify the law by this faith? Not at all! Rather, we uphold the law.

Romans 3:21–31

Paul argues in Romans that all have sinned and are therefore under the wrath of God and the curse of death. Yet God has in his grace accomplished salvation for sinners through the substitutionary death of his Son. In Jesus

Christ there is righteousness, redemption, propitiation, and reconciliation for us. Salvation is accomplished by Christ's own self-offering. But how can we receive this full and free salvation? We have total moral inability and can do nothing to merit salvation. We are dying sinners, wilting under God's wrath. How, then, can we be saved? We are saved by faith in Jesus Christ. *Sola fide* means that we are saved by faith alone, without any works of our own.

What Is Faith?

The word "faith" (*pistis*) appears eight times in this passage and the related verb "believe" (*pisteuō*) appears once. For the first time in this epistle, Paul is telling us in whom we must trust. Romans 3:22 says we must have faith "in Jesus Christ." John often speaks of believing "*into* Jesus Christ." So faith speaks of moving out of ourselves and laying hold of the object of our faith, Jesus Christ. To this purpose John wrote his gospel: "These are written that you may believe that Jesus is the Christ, the Son of God, and that by believing you may have life in his name" (John 20:31).

Faith is self-renouncing and Jesus-trusting. When the Bible says Abraham believed God, it means Abraham put the entire weight of his life—his past, present, and future— upon a firm foundation that will never crumble or give way. Abraham believed in God's promises because God is truth and cannot lie. He trusted in the One who raises the dead and calls into existence things that do not exist.

The words for "believe" in the Old Testament speak of stability, security, and taking refuge in God from all our troubles. We can be secure in God even in the face of death itself. The God we trust in is life and light. The Bible, therefore, speaks about faith that knows, believes, and obeys truth. Such faith rests in God's promises, thanks God for his grace, and works for God's glory. Faith is trust.

Faith can also mean the body of truth that we must believe in (see Gal. 1:23; 1 Tim. 4:1, 6; Jude 3). We believe that Jesus Christ is the eternal Son of God who became incarnate and lived a sinless life. We believe that he created the universe, died for our sins, and was raised for our justification. We believe that Jesus alone is Lord, that he intercedes for us as our great sympathizing high priest, and that he will come again to judge the living and the dead. We believe the gospel as articulated by Paul (1 Cor. 15:1–8).

Our faith rests on the gospel, not on a self-authenticating, mystical experience or dream. God can give us dreams to guide us, but they will not save us. We either receive God's testimony concerning his Son, or we reject it through unbelief. John writes, "The man who has accepted [the testimony of God] has certified that God is truthful" (John 3:33).

When we believe the gospel, we are certifying the truthful nature of God. But what happens when we reject the gospel? "Anyone who believes in the Son of God has this testimony in his heart. Anyone who does not believe God has made him out to be a liar, because he has not believed the testimony God has given about his Son" (1 John 5:10).

The fundamental ingredient of saving faith is orthodoxy; we must believe the gospel. Therefore, churches that do not preach the gospel are not true churches, but entertainment centers that entertain people into damnation. They are, in reality, synagogues of Satan, and what they preach cannot save anyone. The gospel alone points to the person and work of Jesus Christ, our great God and Savior. The object of our faith is God's eternal Son, whom the Father delivered over to death to save his people from their sins. It is Jesus, who is the way and the truth and the life, in whom alone the salvation of the whole world is found, and in whom is redemption (Rom. 3:24).

In What Does Our Faith Rest?

According to the Bible, our faith must rest in God (Mark 11:22), in Christ (Rom. 3:22), in the name of Jesus (Acts 3:16), in Christ's blood (Rom. 3:25), and in the gospel (Phil. 1:27).

Faith Is the Instrumental Cause

Our faith is not the foundation, or basis, of our salvation. In other words, it is not the efficient cause of justification, redemption, propitiation, and reconciliation. The ground of our salvation is the sacrificial death of Jesus Christ. What, then, is faith? Faith is the instrumental cause only. It is the means by which we receive salvation from God as a free gift.

This faith we exercise in Jesus Christ is non-meritorious. John Stott remarks, "Faith is the eye that looks to him, the hand that receives his free gift, the mouth that drinks the living water."[1] B. B. Warfield wrote: "It is not faith that saves, but faith in Jesus Christ. . . . It is not, strictly speaking, even faith in Christ that saves, but Christ that saves through faith."[2] This faith that trusts is the faith of an infant who trusts his mother and sucks her milk freely.

We are saved, not by looking within ourselves or looking to the world around us, but by looking up to Jesus Christ, the object of our faith. Faith is coming to the crucified Christ because he invites us to come. Faith is receiving Christ and calling on his name. It is not resting on anything done in us or by us, but on what is done for us by Jesus Christ. Faith is not our contribution to our own salvation.

---

1   Stott, *Romans: God's Good News,* 117.
2   Quoted by John Murray, *Collected Writings of John Murray,* vol. 2, *Systematic Theology* (Edinburgh: Banner of Truth, 1977), 260.

Faith Is a Gift

We cannot manufacture saving faith; it is a gift granted to us by God. We must believe to be saved, yet this faith is a supernatural gift that does not originate in ourselves.

How can we who are dead in trespasses and sins believe? God must regenerate us and raise us up spiritually. When God saves us, we experience a spiritual resurrection that produces faith. Natural man is incapable of believing the gospel. Faith is a gift of God (Eph. 2:8; Phil. 1:29).

When God sent Paul to Philippi, he preached to a number of women gathered at the river. God opened the heart of Lydia to respond to the gospel, which she did by putting faith in the preached word (Acts 16:14).

Faith Trusts without Doubt

Saving faith trusts in Christ without wavering. Because God is truth, and his promises are true, we can fully trust in him. The psalmist says, "I have trusted in the LORD without wavering" (Ps. 26:1). Faith trusts without doubt. Paul writes,

> Therefore, the promise comes by faith, so that it may be by grace and may be guaranteed to all Abraham's offspring—not only to those who are of the law but also to those who are of the faith of Abraham. . . . He is our father in the sight of God, in whom he believed—the God who gives life to the dead and calls things that are not as though they were. Against all hope, Abraham in hope believed and so became the father of many nations, just as it had been said to him, "So shall your offspring be." Without weakening in his faith, he faced the fact that his body was as good as dead—since he was about a hundred years old—and that Sarah's womb was also dead. Yet he did not waver through unbelief regarding the promise of God, but was strengthened in his faith and gave glory to God, being fully persuaded that God had power to do what he had promised. (Rom. 4:16–21)

Proverbs 3:5 reads, "Trust in the LORD with all your heart and lean not on your own understanding." We trust in God, not in our own native powers. Sarah trusted in her own mind, and the result was Ishmael and much subsequent trouble. That is what happens when we trust in our own understanding.

Faith Is Essential for Salvation

Faith is the *sine qua non* of salvation. All must believe in Jesus Christ to be saved. Like us, the Old Testament saints were saved by faith. The Hebrews writer remarks, "Without faith it is impossible to please God, because anyone who comes to him must believe that he exists and that he rewards those who earnestly seek him" (Heb. 11:6).

What role does work have in our salvation? Jesus says, "The work of God is this: to believe in the one he has sent" (John 6:29). To the Athenians Paul declared, "[God] commands all people everywhere to repent" (Acts 17:30). There is no faith without repentance and no repentance without saving faith.

Where there is genuine faith, there shall also be authentic, godly repentance, which is characterized by deep sorrow for having offended God and a full and free confession of sins. The truly penitent man detests and forsakes his sins. He will make restitution when needed and possible, and he will aim to glorify God by doing what God wants him to do.

Faith Is Directed to Christ

This faith is directed to Christ's person and work. His name is Jesus, "because he will save his people from their sins" (Matt. 1:21). There is no salvation in anyone else (Acts 4:12). Paul writes, "Here is a trustworthy saying that deserves full acceptance: Christ Jesus came into the world to save sinners—of whom I am the worst" (1 Tim. 1:15). Our faith is directed to Christ and his finished work of atonement as well as to his continuing work as our high priest who always makes intercession for us. Paul asks, "Who is he that condemns? Christ Jesus, who died—more than that, who was raised to life—is at the right hand of God and is also interceding for us" (Rom. 8:34).

Faith is directed to Jesus Christ our Savior who, in the offer of the gospel, is not simply making salvation possible but is offering salvation itself, full and free, to be received by faith. He saves every elect sinner.

A Universal Offer of Salvation

This salvation Christ accomplished by his death is offered to all. A universal invitation is given to Jews and Gentiles, rich and poor, male and female. There is no respect of persons; all have sinned and must hear the gospel call.

Paul declares, "*This righteousness from God comes through faith in Jesus Christ to all who believe*" (v. 22). Elsewhere he writes, "I am not ashamed of the gospel, because it is the power of God for the salvation of everyone who believes: first for the Jew, then for the Gentile" (Rom. 1:16).

The Lord himself invites us to believe in him: "Turn to me and be saved, all you ends of the earth; for I am God, and there is no other. . . . Come, all you who are thirsty, come to the waters; and you who have no money, come, buy and eat! Come, buy wine and milk without money and without cost" (Isa. 45:22; 55:1).

Jesus told his disciples to go into all the world and preach the gospel. God also commands all people everywhere to repent. Christ shall come again when the gospel is preached to all nations.

Faith and God's Word

Our faith is born, defined, nourished, and sustained by God's word. God created faith in Lydia through the preached word. Paul tells us, "Faith comes from hearing the message, and the message is heard through the word of Christ" (Rom. 10:17). In other words, faith comes by hearing the gospel preached with all courage and clarity.

Faith is sustained by God's word. As Paul bade farewell to the Ephesian elders, he said, "Now I commit you to God and to the word of his grace, which can build you up and give you an inheritance among all those who are sanctified" (Acts 20:32). The word of God is able to build us up. That is why the devil tries to distract people when the gospel is preached.

No true faith can exist, in other words, without the preaching of the gospel. Thus, true faith does not exist in churches where the word is not preached. Faith in Christ is faith in the word. Without the word, we cannot have even little faith.

Since faith comes by hearing of the word, our faith will grow as we grow in our knowledge of God's word. Therefore, we must be part of a church that declares the gospel and preaches through the entire Bible. We must listen carefully to the preached word and read the Bible daily so that we may have great faith. Older Christians should have stronger faith in Jesus Christ, and younger Christians should consult them, that they may also grow in faith.

Faith Produces Good Works

We are saved by faith in Jesus Christ alone. We believe in Christ so that he may save us, and he saves us apart from any merit of our own, as Paul states: "*But now a righteousness from God, apart from law, has been made known*" (v. 21). We are saved by grace through faith plus nothing.

Yet this faith that saves us also enables us to do good works as evidence of our salvation. Paul writes, "A man is not justified by observing the law, but by faith in Jesus Christ. . . . For in Christ Jesus neither circumcision nor uncircumcision has any value. The only thing that counts is faith expressing itself through love" (Gal. 2:16; 5:6).

Faith without works is a corpse. It is not true saving faith; rather, it is the faith of demons (James 2:19). Demons believe, yet their end will be the lake of fire. Theirs is a dead faith, like the faith of the second and third soil-hearers of the gospel (Matt. 13). It is the faith of Achan, King Saul, Judas, Ananias and Sapphira, Simon Magus, and Demas.

True faith results in active obedience to God's word. Paul declares, "Through [Christ] and for his name's sake, we received grace and apostleship to call people from among all the Gentiles to the obedience that comes from faith" (Rom. 1:5).

Our good works prove that our salvation is by faith alone apart from works. They are the evidence that we are true people of God. For example, notice the language Paul uses to Timothy on the issue of a man's responsibility for his family: "If anyone does not provide for his relatives, and especially for his immediate family, he has denied the faith and is worse than an unbeliever" (1 Tim. 5:8).

This is also true of a man who does not love his wife. His faith is false. Paul says we are created in Christ Jesus unto good works, which God has foreordained that we should walk in them (Eph. 2:10). Jesus himself said, "By their fruit you will recognize them" (Matt. 7:20).

We are saved by faith and must live by faith. We do not come to Jesus by faith first and then abandon our faith to live by sight. We must always live by faith in God. Faith unites us to Christ, and by faith we abide in Christ, who is wisdom, righteousness, sanctification, and redemption.

Elements of Faith

Saving faith has three constitutive elements: knowledge (*notitia*), agreement (*assensus*), and trust (*fiducia*). Knowledge of the gospel leads us to conviction (i.e., active agreement with the truth), and such conviction leads us to personal trust in Jesus Christ.

The first element of faith is knowledge. Christian faith is not pious ignorance. Nor is it trusting in oneself, trusting in one's positive thinking, or trusting in one's church. True faith is trusting in Jesus Christ to be saved. Therefore we need knowledge of the gospel of Christ. Without knowledge we cannot have true faith, because true faith is born, defined, and nourished by the word of God. Faith comes by hearing the gospel facts preached by one commissioned and sent by Christ.

Roman Catholics claim that biblical knowledge is not necessary, as long as one trusts implicitly in the Roman church. Such people would say, "You trust the church and the church will relate to Christ on your behalf." But we say, "We must trust in Christ directly." James M. Boice relates a story:

> A man was being interviewed by a group of church officers before being taken into membership. They asked him what he believed about salvation, and he replied that he believed what the church believed.
>
> "But what does the church believe?" they probed.
>
> "The church believes what I believe," he answered.
>
> They tried again: "Just what do you and the church believe?"
>
> The man thought this over for a moment and then replied, "We believe the same thing."[3]

---

3   Boice, *Romans*, vol. 1, *Justification by Faith*, 389.

Christianity is a reasonable faith based on knowledge. It is not a leap into the darkness of irrationality. We must base our faith on information. Churches, therefore, must give knowledge of the gospel that will lead people to faith. Our faith is based on God's revelation of what he has done in Jesus Christ.

We can liken these elements of faith to stages of courtship. When a woman begins to date a person, she wants to collect information. Who is this person? Who are his parents? What type of job history does he have? Does he have money in the bank? Does he have any spiritual character? Dating is the time for the primacy of the intellect. She is merely gathering information.

The second element is agreement, *assensus*. Our knowledge of the facts of the gospel now moves us to conviction, which means we agree that the gospel is true—that Jesus Christ is Savior and Lord, that he died for our sins, and that we can be saved by trusting in him. This is similar to the second stage in dating; it is a movement of the heart. At this point a girl will agree that this man is handsome, intelligent, of excellent character, healthy, and hardworking. She comes to the conclusion that this person can be an excellent husband for her, and she can live with him all of her life in great joy.

But *assensus* is not trust. Conviction must move to trust—*fiducia*. Otherwise, it is dead faith, the faith of Judas, the devil's faith. As we said, the devil is orthodox. He believes in the Scriptures, has knowledge of God, and even agrees with this knowledge. That is why the third aspect of faith is so important.

Faith in its essence is commitment to Christ that we may be saved. We must trust in Jesus Christ alone for our salvation, entrusting ourselves to him now and forever. We do not trust in ourselves or in any human or angelic resources, but in Jesus Christ alone as Savior and submit to him as Lord, that we may be saved. We trust in Jesus as an infant trusts in his mother. We declare, "Jesus is *my* Savior, *my* Lord, *my* Shepherd, *my* Healer." This speaks of the third stage in dating: making a lifetime commitment to one's spouse in marriage. Jesus is our bridegroom and we are his beloved bride (Rev. 19:6–9). By faith we are united with him. All his assets are ours; all our liabilities are his.

Do You Live by Faith Alone?

God has accomplished salvation by the sacrifice of his Son. A great feast has been made ready for all dying sinners. All the fitness God requires is for us to see our need of Christ, for Jesus saves only sinners. We must come by faith; no merit is required.

Heed the words of John Owen:

> This is somewhat of the word which he now speaks unto you: Why will ye die? why will ye perish? why will ye not have compassion on your own souls? Can your hearts endure, or can your hands be strong, in the day of wrath that is approaching? . . . Look unto me, and be saved; come unto me, and I will ease you of all sins, sorrows, fears, burdens, and give rest to your souls. Come, I entreat you; lay aside all procrastinations, all delays; put me off no more; eternity lies at the door . . . do not so hate me as that you would rather perish than accept of deliverance by me.
>
> These and the like things doth the Lord Christ continually declare, proclaim, plead and urge on the souls of sinners. . . . He doth it in the preaching of the word, as if he were present with you, stood amongst you, and spake personally to every one of you. . . . He hath appointed the ministers of the gospel to appear before you, and to deal with you in his stead, avowing as his own the invitations that are given you in his name.[4]

---

4   Quoted by Wayne Grudem, *Systematic Theology* (Grand Rapids: Zondervan Publishing House, 1994), 712.

What must we do to be saved? Believe on the Lord Jesus Christ and you will be saved.

Application Questions

1) What is faith? How does it relate to salvation?

2) As long as we just believe, does it matter in whom we believe?

3) How can we know that we have saving faith?

6

Soli Deo Gloria

27Where, then, is boasting? It is excluded. On what principle? On that of observing the law? No, but on that of faith. 28For we maintain that a man is justified by faith apart from observing the law. 29Is God the God of Jews only? Is he not the God of Gentiles too? Yes, of Gentiles too, 30since there is only one God, who will justify the circumcised by faith and the uncircumcised through that same faith. 31Do we, then, nullify the law by this faith? Not at all! Rather, we uphold the law.

Romans 3:27–31

In Romans 3:21–26, Paul spoke about God's plan of salvation through faith in Christ alone. Now he makes the logical connection: If salvation for sinners is by grace alone (*sola gratia*) through faith in Christ alone (*sola fide*), then the saved sinner must give glory to God alone (*soli Deo gloria*). A dying beggar who has been given a feast by a gracious king cannot boast that he deserved this royal feast. He must give all the glory to the king. In the same way, the saved saints shall praise God forever, proclaiming: "Salvation belongs to our God, who sits on the throne, and to the Lamb" (Rev. 7:10).

Consider who we were when we met Jesus Christ. First, we were impotent to save ourselves. No man can save himself, even though all other religions speak in terms of self-salvation. Second, we were sinners who transgressed God's holy laws and thus dishonored him. Third, we were ungodly and therefore unrighteous fools who said in our hearts that there is no God. Fourth, we were enemies of God, for sin is essentially enmity toward God. Yet we were loved by the Father, who sent his Son to die for us. Away with all human pride! Instead, let us praise God in all humility.

The proper response to our eternal salvation is not boasting but rather praising the triune God who saved us. In Romans 3:27–31, Paul teaches us that salvation by grace through faith in Jesus Christ excludes three things: boasting, discrimination, and lawlessness.

Justification Excludes Boasting

Justification by grace through faith excludes all boasting: *"Where, then, is boasting? It is excluded. On what principle? On that of observing the law? No, but on that of faith"* (v. 27).

Pride is the sin that made Lucifer the devil: "How you have fallen from heaven, O morning star, son of the dawn! You have been cast down to the earth, you who once laid low the nations! You said in your heart, 'I will ascend to heaven; I will raise my throne above the stars of God; I will sit enthroned on the mount of assembly, on the utmost heights of the sacred mountain. I will ascend above the tops of the clouds; I will make myself like the Most High'" (Isa. 14:12–14).

The essence of arrogance is for man to dethrone God and establish himself as God. But God declares to such usurpers: "I will rise up against them. . . . I will cut off from Babylon her name and survivors, her offspring and descendants. . . . I will turn her into a place for owls and into swampland; I will sweep her with the broom of destruction" (Isa. 14:22–23). The Lord will not tolerate human arrogance.

C. S. Lewis, in *Mere Christianity*, speaks about pride:

> There is one vice of which no man in the world is free;
> which every one in the world loathes when he sees
> it in someone else; and of which hardly any people,
> except Christians, ever imagine that they are guilty
> themselves. I have heard people admit that they are bad-
> tempered, or that they cannot keep their heads about
> girls or drink, or even that they are cowards. I do not
> think I have ever heard anyone who was not a Christian
> accuse himself of this vice. And at the same time I have
> very seldom met anyone, who was not a Christian, who
> showed the slightest mercy to it in others. There is no
> fault which makes a man more unpopular, and no fault
> which we are more unconscious of in ourselves. And
> the more we have it in ourselves, the more we dislike it
> in others. The vice I am talking of is Pride.[1]

The Jews were boasters who constantly bragged about
their race and religious privileges. They considered
themselves holy and looked down on others, calling them
unclean dogs. Paul speaks about their bragging: "Now you,
if you call yourself a Jew; if you rely on the law and brag
about your relationship to God . . . You who brag about
the law, do you dishonor God by breaking the law? . . . If,
in fact, Abraham was justified by works, he had something
to boast about—but not before God" (Rom. 2:17, 23; 4:2).

Elsewhere he lists the privileges the Jews boasted about:
"Theirs is the adoption as sons; theirs the divine glory, the
covenants, the receiving of the law, the temple worship
and the promises. Theirs are the patriarchs, and from
them is traced the human ancestry of Christ, who is God
over all, forever praised! Amen" (Rom. 9:4–5). John the
Baptist rebuked such boasters: "Do not think you can say
to yourselves, 'We have Abraham as our father.' I tell you
that out of these stones God can raise up children for
Abraham" (Matt. 3:9).

---

1   C. S. Lewis, *Mere Christianity* (New York: Macmillan Company,
     1971), 108–9.

Jesus spoke of the boastful pride of a Pharisee: "To some who were confident of their own righteousness and looked down on everybody else, Jesus told this parable: 'Two men went up to the temple to pray, one a Pharisee and the other a tax collector. The Pharisee stood up and prayed about himself: "God, I thank you that I am not like other men—robbers, evildoers, adulterers—or even like this tax collector. I fast twice a week and give a tenth of all I get""'" (Luke 18:9–12).

Consider the words of another Pharisee, who became a battle-scarred veteran of the cross: "If anyone else thinks he has reasons to put confidence in the flesh, I have more: circumcised on the eighth day, of the people of Israel, of the tribe of Benjamin, a Hebrew of Hebrews; in regard to the law, a Pharisee; as for zeal, persecuting the church; as for legalistic righteousness, faultless" (Phil. 3:4–6).

Such bragging, however, was not only the business of the Jews; Gentiles boasted also. Paul writes of the Gentiles, "Although they claimed to be wise, they became fools. . . . They exchanged the truth of God for a lie, and worshiped and served created things rather than the Creator. . . . Furthermore, since they did not think it worthwhile to retain the knowledge of God, he gave them over to a depraved mind. . . . [They are] slanderers, God-haters, insolent, arrogant and boastful" (Rom. 1:22, 25, 28, 30). Paul elsewhere remarks,

> For the message of the cross is foolishness to those who are perishing, but to us who are being saved it is the power of God. For it is written: 'I will destroy the wisdom of the wise; the intelligence of the intelligent I will frustrate.' Where is the wise man? Where is the scholar? Where is the philosopher of this age? Has not God made foolish the wisdom of the world? . . . Brothers, think of what you were when you were called. Not many of you were wise by human standards; not many were influential; not many were of noble birth. But God chose the foolish things of the world to shame the wise; God chose the weak things of the world to shame the strong. He chose

the lowly things of this world and the despised things—
and the things that are not—to nullify the things that
are, so that no one may boast before him. . . . Therefore,
as it is written: "Let him who boasts boast in the Lord."
(1 Cor. 1:18–20, 26–29, 31)

Though Jews and Gentiles may boast, the Bible clearly
teaches that sinful man is not justified by any human
merit, but only by the merit of Jesus Christ. As Paul writes,
"Therefore no one will be declared righteous in his sight
by observing the law. . . . But now a righteousness from
God apart from the law has been made known. . . . For
we maintain that a man is justified by faith apart from
observing the law" (Rom. 3:20, 21, 28). Our own works only
can condemn us to hell; the work of Christ alone saves us.

Paul gives the reason God sent his Son to be a propitiation
for our sins: "He did it to demonstrate his justice at the
present time, so as to be just and the one who justifies
those who have faith in Jesus" (Rom. 3:26). The efficient
cause of justification *by works* is what man does, while the
efficient cause of justification *by faith* is what Christ does.
Our faith is extraspective (looking always to Christ alone),
not introspective (looking to ourselves). Paul thus declares,
"We live by faith, not by sight" (2 Cor. 5:7).

Even Abraham, the father of all believers, had no cause
to boast in himself, but believed in God and was justified
(Rom. 4:1–3). Salvation by Christ's death excludes all
human boasting. The cross has done it all. Many of our
great Christian hymns highlight the biblical truth that
God alone deserves all the credit for our salvation:

Jesus paid it all; all to him we owe.

and

Amazing grace, how sweet the sound,
that saved a wretch like me.

What about our good works of obedience to God? All our good works are the effect of God's grace. Jesus taught that a branch can do nothing unless it is united to the vine and lives by its life: "Because I live, you also will live" (John 14:19). Paul also argues this point: "God is able to make all grace abound to you, so that in all things at all times, having all that you need, you will abound in every good work" (2 Cor. 9:8). We are God's workmanship, "created in Christ Jesus unto good works, which God has foreordained that we should walk in them" (Eph. 2:10, KJV), but we do all these works by grace. And if they are by grace, where is our boasting?

Yet the saints of God can boast, both here and in heaven. We boast in God and give him all the glory, as Paul did: "Therefore, as it is written: 'Let him who boasts boast in the Lord'" (1 Cor. 1:31). Jeremiah speaks of this: "This is what the Lord says: 'Let not the wise man boast of his wisdom or the strong man boast of his strength or the rich man boast of his riches, but let him who boasts boast about this: that he understands and knows me, that I am the Lord, who exercises kindness, justice and righteousness on earth, for in these I delight,' declares the Lord" (Jer. 9:23–24).

If you still want to boast, consider these words of Paul: "For who makes you different from anyone else? What do you have that you did not receive? And if you did receive it, why do you boast as though you did not?" (1 Cor. 4:7). Therefore, let us pour contempt upon all our pride and sing praise to our gracious God.

Justification Excludes Discrimination

The second thing that justification by grace through faith excludes is all sinful discrimination. We can make rules against discrimination, but it resides deep within every human heart. But there is no such discrimination with God; all have sinned and fall short of his glory, and all need to be saved by Christ.

"For we maintain that a man is justified by faith apart from observing the law" (v. 28). The Greek text uses *anthrōpos* as the word for "man," meaning *every* man, both Jew and Gentile. The only way of salvation for all people is through faith in Jesus Christ. In other words, man is justified by faith, not by his works. Either one tries to save himself by his good works, which is true of all other religions, or he is saved by faith in the work of Jesus on the cross.

Then Paul adduces the argument that God is one, and that this one God is the God of both Jews and Gentiles: *"Is God the God of Jews only? Is he not the God of Gentiles too? Yes, of Gentiles too, since there is only one God, who will justify the circumcised by faith and the uncircumcised through that same faith"* (vv. 29–30). Paul is using the monotheistic doctrine of the Jews to defeat their arrogance and exclusivism.

This idea that God is one is found throughout the Scriptures. Moses declared, "Hear, O Israel: The LORD our God, the LORD is one" (Deut. 6:4; see also Isa. 43:11; 45:5, 21–22). The psalmist exhorts: "Sing to the LORD a new song; sing to the LORD, all the earth" (Ps. 96:1). Abraham asks the Lord, "Will not the Judge of all the earth do right?" (Gen. 18:25). If God is one, then he is God of all people, and there can therefore be only one way of salvation. There is one God and one Savior.

Man is always creating differences, whether based on race, income, gender, or rank. But Paul declares in Romans 3:22–23, "There is no difference, for all have sinned and come short of the glory of God." Just as there are not many gods, so there are also not many ways of salvation—one way for the Jews and another way for the Gentiles. There is no discrimination in the way sinners are saved. That is why Paul so boldly proclaims, "I am not ashamed of the gospel, because it is the power of God for the salvation of everyone who believes: first for the Jew, then for the Gentile" (Rom. 1:16).

This way of salvation was God's plan from all eternity. The Lord told Abraham, "I will bless those who bless you, and whoever curses you I will curse; and all peoples on earth will be blessed through you" (Gen. 12:3). We also read, "And through your offspring [meaning Jesus Christ] all nations on earth will be blessed, because you have obeyed me" (Gen. 22:18). Jesus confirmed this to his disciples: "This is what is written: The Christ will suffer and rise from the dead on the third day, and repentance and forgiveness of sins will be preached in his name to all nations, beginning at Jerusalem" (Luke 24:46–47).

Paul also speaks of this plan: "Consider Abraham: 'He believed God, and it was credited to him as righteousness.' Understand, then, that those who believe are children of Abraham. The Scripture foresaw that God would justify the Gentiles by faith, and announced the gospel in advance to Abraham: 'All nations will be blessed through you.' So those who have faith are blessed along with Abraham, the man of faith" (Gal. 3:6–9).

There is one God, one people, and one way of salvation through faith in the one Savior, Jesus Christ. Jesus said, "I am the way and the truth and the life" (John 14:6). Peter declares that there is salvation in no other (Acts 4:12). Paul explains that God is one and is God of all, and this one God has one way of salvation (1 Tim. 2:5–6). At the foot of the cross, we are all equal. There is no difference, whether in sin, condemnation, or salvation. God pardons the sins of Jews and Gentiles alike, making them all saints and sons of God. All other ways of salvation are false because they refuse to recognize Jesus as the Son of God.

Sinful discrimination in the church, therefore, should be outlawed. How many churches are organized by ethnicity? I read of a situation in which a black family visited a predominantly white church and the pastor later visited the black family and suggested that they would be more comfortable in a black church several miles away. But a church that discriminates in such a way is not a church of Christ. Paul insists that the people of God consist of believing Jews and Gentiles. Both circumcised and uncircumcised are saved by faith in Christ. The church is an international body of believers from all tribes and languages and nations, all colors in the spectrum.

Jesus Christ destroys sinful discrimination. Paul speaks of this:

> Therefore, remember that formerly you who are Gentiles by birth and called 'uncircumcised' by those who call themselves 'the circumcision' . . . remember that at that time you were separate from Christ, excluded from citizenship in Israel and foreigners to the covenants of the promise, without hope and without God in the world. But now in Christ Jesus you who once were far away have been brought near through the blood of Christ.

> For he himself is our peace, who has made the two one and has destroyed the barrier, the dividing wall of hostility, by abolishing in his flesh the law with its commandments and regulations. His purpose was to create in himself one new man out of the two, thus making peace, and in this one body to reconcile both of them to God through the cross, by which he put to death their hostility. He came and preached peace to you who were far away and peace to those who were near. For through him we both have access to the Father by one Spirit.

> Consequently, you are no longer foreigners and aliens, but fellow citizens with God's people and members of God's household, built on the foundation of the apostles and prophets, with Christ Jesus himself as the chief cornerstone. In him the whole building is joined together and rises to become a holy temple in the Lord. And in him you too are being built together to become a dwelling in which God lives by his Spirit. (Eph. 2:11–22; see also Eph. 3:6; 4:4–6)

Elsewhere he writes, "You are all sons of God through faith in Christ Jesus, for all of you who were baptized into Christ have clothed yourselves with Christ. There is neither Jew nor Greek, slave nor free, male nor female, for you are all one in Christ Jesus. If you belong to Christ, then you are Abraham's seed, and heirs according to the promise" (Gal. 3:26–29).

I was born into an upper-caste Syrian Orthodox church in India, and my family did not associate with anyone of a lower caste. But when the Holy Spirit was poured out in that area, God destroyed all such human barriers. I remember going as a young boy with my father and our pastor to visit an "untouchable" who had come to know Christ. We sat on the ground in this pariah's hut, ate what he gave us, and experienced true biblical fellowship. When the Holy Spirit was poured out, our deeply embedded distinctions were abolished.

We all belong to one family—we have one heavenly Father, and are brothers and sisters in Jesus Christ. We all are saints of God and can all approach God in the name of Jesus. John Stott says: "All who believe in Jesus belong to the same family and should be eating at the same table. That is what Paul's doctrine of justification by faith is all about."[2] Yet we must always fight against the sinful impulse to discriminate. Even Peter, who was taught this lesson of oneness in Christ in Acts 10, failed to practice it later in the church at Antioch. Paul had to rebuke him publicly for his discriminatory actions (Gal. 2:11ff).

Justification Excludes Lawlessness

The third thing that justification by grace through faith excludes is lawlessness, or antinomianism. Far too many evangelicals today consider law and grace to be

---

2   Stott, *Romans: God's Good News*, 120.

antithetical. In fact, they proudly assert that they are living by grace because they do not obey God's law.

Paul deals with this in the last verse of our text: *"Do we, then, nullify the law by this faith? Not at all! Rather, we uphold the law"* (v. 31). The argument goes like this: If justification is not by the works of the law but by faith in Jesus Christ, then what is the use of the law? Is the law worthless? Does the faith principle nullify the law? The answer is, "By no means!" We do not annul the law; instead, we uphold the law. The law is never antithetical to grace. Let us look at certain reasons:

1. The law reveals the character of God, especially his holiness. The law was given by God; therefore, it is holy, righteous, good, and spiritual (Rom. 7:12).
2. The law reveals our character. Like a mirror, it shows our moral filth (Rom. 3:20; 7:7).
3. The law itself testifies to salvation by grace (Rom. 3:21).
4. The goal of the law is Jesus Christ (Rom. 10:4).
5. Jesus came to fulfill the law in behalf of us (see Matt. 3:15; 5:17–18; Gal. 4:4–6; Heb. 5:8). Salvation is by the works of Christ's obedience to God's law, so salvation for us can be found through faith in Christ, who obeyed the law. Dr. Martyn Lloyd-Jones says, "What the Apostle maintains here is that God's way of declaring those who believe in Christ to be righteous honours and establishes the Law."[3]
6. God did not give the law to impart life to us (Gal. 3:21).
7. The law condemns us, yet it also points us to Jesus for salvation. It acts like John the Baptist, who said, "Look, the Lamb of God, who takes away the sin of the world!" (John 1:29). The law leads us to Christ (Gal. 3:23–25).
8. Grace enables us to keep the moral law of God. Jesus said, "If you love me, you will obey what I command" (John 14:15). Paul writes, "Let no debt remain outstanding, except the continuing debt to love one another, for he who loves his fellowman

---

3   D. Martyn Lloyd-Jones, *Romans*, vol. 3, *An Exposition of Romans 3:20–4:25: Atonement and Justification* (Grand Rapids: Zondervan, 1971), 144.

has fulfilled the law. The commandments, 'Do not commit adultery,' 'Do not murder,' 'Do not steal,' 'Do not covet,' and whatever other commandment there may be, are summed up in this one rule: 'Love your neighbor as yourself.' Love does no harm to its neighbor. Therefore love is the fulfillment of the law" (Rom. 13:8–10). Jesus said the first commandment is, "Love the Lord your God with all your heart and with all your soul and with all your mind." The second is this: "Love your neighbor as yourself." All the Law and the Prophets hang on these two commandments (Matt. 22:37–40). Those who are justified by faith will keep God's commandments by God's enabling grace.

9. The law pronounces judgment on all violators of God's law. "The wrath of God is being revealed from heaven against all the godlessness and wickedness of men" (Rom. 1:18; see also Rom. 6:23; Ezek. 18:20).

Conclusion

If you have not trusted in Jesus Christ alone and have not been redeemed by Christ's death, then the law of God condemns you. If you are not justified by the Father on the basis of the righteousness of Christ alone, then God's wrath is abiding on you. Soon you shall die in your sins and enter into God's eternal judgment. I pray that you will recognize the seriousness of this danger and repent of your sins, believe in Jesus Christ who fully obeyed the law for you, and be saved forever.

To those who are justified by faith: Let us be humble and not boast in anything except in the cross of Christ. Let us worship God all of life and live for his glory. Let us not discriminate, but let us love one another, knowing that we are equally sinners, saints, and sons of God in God's only Son. Let us lay down our lives for our brothers.

Finally, let us uphold the law of God by his grace. Away with all Christian antinomianism, autonomy, and cheap grace! God has made us who were his enemies into lovers of God, and love fulfills God's law. Let us prove daily that we are God's children by obeying our heavenly Father exactly, immediately, and with great joy as the Holy Spirit enables us.

Application Questions

1) Why does God's salvation in Jesus Christ exclude human boasting?

2) Why does God's salvation exclude ongoing lawlessness?

3) Are you prepared to stand before God and give an account for what you have done about the Savior whom he has sent?

Epilogue

In Romans 3:21–26 we have the very heart of the gospel message spoken by God to sinners like you and me. I have explained from this passage how God in Jesus Christ mercifully accomplished the salvation of unrighteous men and women while at the same time exalting his own perfect righteousness. At the cross, love and justice kissed. This surely is good news!

Yet this is not good news for everyone, for it is news that benefits only those who believe the gospel and obey its summons. The gospel saves only those who realize that they are evil in God's sight, and that they urgently need the mercy, forgiveness, and deliverance from sin that Jesus Christ offers.

The Lord Jesus himself emphasized this in his teaching. In response to a question regarding some Jews who were killed, he replied, "Do you think that these Galileans were worse sinners than all the other Galileans because they suffered this way? I tell you, no! But unless you repent, you too will all perish" (Luke 13:2–3). Soon afterwards, he drove home the same point: "Make every effort to enter through the narrow door, because many, I tell you, will try to enter and will not be able to" (Luke 13:24).

And in his parable of the Great Banquet, Jesus exposed the all-too-common response to the gospel call: "A certain man was preparing a great banquet and invited many guests. At the time of the banquet he sent his servant to tell those who had been invited, 'Come, for everything is now ready.' But they all alike began to make excuses" (Luke 14:16–18). Jesus' subsequent warning is a warning to us all: "Then the owner of the house became angry" (Luke 14:21).

The importance of Jesus' teaching is clear. Now that you know the gospel message, now that the gospel invitation has been extended to you, you must immediately come to Jesus Christ in repentance and faith, forsaking your sins and entrusting yourself to this risen Lord and Savior forever. You must not delay; now is the time of God's favor, now is the day of salvation (2 Cor. 6:2).

To say "No" to the gospel is to tell God that you are good and do not need Jesus. To say "No" is to tell God that he is a liar. To say "No" is to refuse God's own gracious summons, and such a refusal will only add to the punishment you will experience for all eternity. The Father's eternal decree is that every knee shall bow and every tongue confess that Jesus Christ is Lord (Phil. 2:10–11). To fail to make this confession is to mock God and his Son.

Therefore I urge you, say "Yes" to the Lord of the gospel! Flee to Jesus Christ in faith, and he will receive you graciously, as he promised: "Come to me, all you who are weary and burdened, and I will give you rest. Take my yoke upon you and learn from me, for I am gentle and humble in heart, and you will find rest for your souls. For my yoke is easy and my burden is light" (Matt. 11:28–30). Do so today, that we together might enjoy and celebrate forever God's salvation that "comes through faith in Jesus Christ to all who believe" (Rom. 3:22).

CONTENT OUTLINE OF
GOOD NEWS FOR ALL PEOPLE

I. God's Diagnosis: <u>Divine Diagnosis of Man's Heart</u>
    (ch. 1), Rom. 3:9–20

    a. Each of us is a sinner who will experience
       God's righteous judgment

    b. Sin is universal—all men are under its power

    c. Sin resides in the heart—it is internal, not
       external to man

        i. Sin twists the mind—no man
          understands God

        ii. Sin twists the will—no man seeks God

    d. Sin is lawlessness—no man keeps God's law

        i. Sin twists conduct—no man does what is
          righteous and good in God's sight

        ii. Sin poisons the tongue—man uses his
           mouth to curse God and injure others

    e. Sin brings divine judgment because no man
       is righteous in God's sight

II. God's Prescription: His accomplishment of
     salvation in behalf of sinners, Rom. 3:21–26

   a. <u>Justification by Grace</u> (ch. 2)—God's salvation:
       the justification of the sinner

       i. A righteousness of God is now revealed in
           the life, death, and resurrection of Jesus

       ii. This righteousness of God is apart from
            man's efforts

       iii. This righteousness of God was promised
             in the Old Testament

       iv. This righteousness of God is what justifies
            the sinner in God's sight

            1. This justification is a legal declaration
                that our sins are forgiven and God's
                righteousness is ours

            2. The only source of justification is
                God's grace

            3. The ground of justification is the
                person and work of Christ

   b. <u>Redemption in Christ</u> (ch. 3)—God's
       salvation: the redemption of the sinner

       i. This redemption sets sinners free from
           their bondage to Satan, sin, the law, and
           God's just punishment

       ii. This redemption cannot be accomplished
            by the sinner himself

       iii. This redemption was accomplished by our
             kinsman-redeemer, Jesus Christ

       1. The redemption price was the death of Christ on Calvary

       2. Redemption has two components: the present and the future

       3. Redemption brings numerous blessings

  c. Salvation as Propitiation (ch. 4)—God's salvation: the propitiation of God's just wrath

     i. This propitiation results from a sacrifice that satisfies the justice of God and so appeases his wrath

     ii. This propitiation took place at God the Father's initiative

     iii. This propitiation is the result of Jesus' atoning death on the cross for sinners

     iv. This propitiation publicly vindicates God's justice

     v. Propitiation results in:

       1. Forgiveness of sins

       2. Access to God

       3. No condemnation

III. Man's Responsibility: Sinners are saved by faith alone in Jesus Christ alone

  a. Sola Fide (ch. 5), Rom. 3:21–31—Faith is the means by which we receive salvation from God as a free gift

  b. This faith is non-meritorious; it is a gift from God

    c. This faith is essential; without it salvation is impossible

    d. This faith is directed to the person and work of Christ

    e. This faith comes by hearing the gospel

    f. This faith produces works of obedience to God

    g. Faith consists of:

        i. Knowledge

        ii. Agreement

        iii. Trust

IV.   God's Ultimate Purpose: <u>Soli Deo Gloria</u> (ch. 6), Rom. 3:27–31

    a. Saved sinners must boast in God, not in themselves

    b. Saved sinners must not discriminate against others

    c. Saved sinners must not live lawless lives that dishonor God

Grace and Glory Ministries

Grace and Glory Ministries is an extension of Grace Valley Christian Center. We are committed to the teaching of God's infallible word. It is our mission to proclaim the whole gospel to the whole world for the building up of the whole body of Christ.

For more information about Grace Valley Christian Center, or to obtain additional copies of this book, visit www.gracevalley.org.